AFGHANISTAN

THE SOVIET INVASION IN PERSPECTIVE

Anthony Arnold

Hoover International Studies
Richard F. Staar, general editor

AFGHANISTAN
The Soviet Invasion in Perspective

HOOVER INTERNATIONAL STUDIES
Richard F. Staar, director

THE PANAMA CANAL CONTROVERSY
Paul B. Ryan

THE IMPERIALIST REVOLUTIONARIES
Hugh Seton-Watson

SOUTH AFRICA: WAR, REVOLUTION, OR PEACE?
L. H. Gann and Peter Duignan

TWO CHINESE STATES
Ramon Myers, editor

THE CLOUDED LENS: PERSIAN GULF SECURITY
James Noyes

SOVIET STRATEGY FOR NUCLEAR WAR
Joseph Douglass, Jr., and Amoretta Hoeber

SCIENCE, TECHNOLOGY AND CHINA'S DRIVE FOR
MODERNIZATION
Richard P. Suttmeier

THE END OF THE TITO ERA: YUGOSLAVIA'S DILEMMAS
Slobodan Stanković

WAITING FOR A "PEARL HARBOR"
Tetsuya Kataoka

AFGHANISTAN: THE SOVIET INVASION IN PERSPECTIVE
Anthony Arnold

AFGHANISTAN

The Soviet Invasion in Perspective

ANTHONY ARNOLD

HOOVER INSTITUTION PRESS

Stanford University, Stanford, California

COVER PHOTOGRAPH: Photri

The Hoover Institution on War, Revolution and Peace, founded at Stanford University in 1919 by the late President Herbert Hoover, is an interdisciplinary research center for advanced study on domestic and international affairs in the twentieth century. The views expressed in its publications are entirely those of the authors and do not necessarily reflect the views of the staff, officers, or Board of Overseers of the Hoover Institution.

Hoover Press Publication 251

Design by P. Kelley Baker

To my friends the Afghans
As in the past,
enshalla,
Your pride, courage, and individualism
will prevail

Contents

Editor's Foreword

From being one of the least known countries in the world, Afghanistan has been catapulted into the world limelight since the Soviet invasion of December 1979. It is premature to assess the full significance of that event, if for no other reason than the fact that its ultimate success remains in doubt. The Afghans, against all odds and logic, go on fighting. USSR troops, after a year of battle, appear no closer to victory than they were at the outset.

It is not too early, however, to observe and comment on the events that led up to the invasion or to point up some of the unique features of the situation that already have become apparent.

In invading Afghanistan, the Soviet Union appeared to be setting a new and more aggressive pattern in its foreign policies. If one compares certain military occupations by Stalin in 1939 and 1940 (eastern Poland, the Baltic states, parts of Finland), one must acknowledge that all of these lands once had belonged, rightly or wrongly, to tsarist Russia. Despite opposition to USSR rule by the vast majority of their populations, Stalin, as de facto heir to the tsars, could lay claim to at least some historical right to the territories.

Afghanistan, by contrast, had never before been conquered or occupied (except for temporary cross-border bridgeheads) by either tsarist or Soviet troops. The invasion thus represents a precedent of considerable significance, one that seems to presage a willingness by the USSR to project its military power abroad with less constraint than in the past.

That it had decided to do so cannot be explained by any single factor. Though one may argue as to the relative importance each of the following considerations held in Soviet eyes (indeed the relative weight of each probably differed in the minds of principal Kremlin decision-makers), all undoubtedly played some role:

Changing Correlation of Forces   Soviet perceptions of its own military power and growing relative strength vis-à-vis the West clearly represented an important factor. The temptation to experiment with USSR armed forces directly (rather than via proxies such as the Cuban troops in Africa) must have been strong. One can even speculate that ranking Soviet military officers could have wanted to expose their units to combat conditions as a means of giving them real life experience obtainable in no other way.

Strategic Importance of Afghanistan   Though a poor country, Afghanistan's strategic location—at the gateway to Middle East oil reserves, close to warm water ports, and on the flanks of China and Pakistan—provided both economic and geopolitical incentives for intervention.

Ideological Commitment   Once having accepted Afghanistan into the ranks of the socialist family of nations, the USSR was obligated under the Brezhnev Doctrine to prevent any return to a noncommunist form of government.

One can imagine each of the key Politburo members accepting one or another of the above arguments as the dominant consideration: Brezhnev, the economic and geopolitical aspects; Ustinov, the military; Suslov, the ideological.

Probably none of these, however, would have justified intervention if it had not been for one final consideration: the almost certain belief that there would be no effective American response to the invasion. United States armed forces were far away from the region, so they could not act as a deterrent. Perhaps even more important was the psychological element, namely, the apparent absence of any readiness to oppose the USSR. If there had been any residual Soviet concern about a possible American reaction, it is likely that it lost all credibility when the United States failed to respond swiftly and resolutely to the taking of American hostages by Iranian students in November, less than eight weeks before the invasion of Afghanistan.

Nevertheless, in the year that has elapsed, the effects of the invasion itself have been to reverse the trend toward neo-isolationism in the United States. National defense became a key issue in the 1980 presidential election, there has been renewed American recognition of Soviet expansionist ambitions, and there is stronger resolve to oppose them. Some of the specific costs to the USSR probably were foreseen in the Kremlin: the embargo on grain and advanced technology, the failure of SALT II to pass the Senate, and the curtailment of the scientific exchange program. Others perhaps may not have been anticipated: the Olympic boycott, the strength of the UN General Assembly vote against the USSR (104 to 18), and augmentation of the effects of the U.S. grain embargo due to poor harvests elsewhere in the world and especially in the USSR itself.

If the above elements continue to work against Soviet interests, that fact perhaps can be attributed more than anything else to the determination of the Afghan population to go on fighting despite the odds against it. Had the USSR succeeded in a Czechoslovakia-type rapid and bloodless occupation, the chances for sustained Western sanctions would have been much reduced. Instead, the resistance continues to eat away at Soviet strength, prestige, and credibility. As a result, Afghanistan has become a pivotal issue not only for 1980 but perhaps for the decade ahead, with ever broadening ramifications for the USSR, other Soviet-controlled countries, the West, and all of Asia.

This book examines the events that led to Soviet armed intervention. The progression from economic to political to military interference in order to establish Soviet control is not limited to Afghanistan. Perhaps an early identification of similar techniques employed elsewhere by the USSR may also lead to timely deterrence against future Soviet resort to military force.

Richard F. Staar

Director of International Studies
Hoover Institution

Preface

Since the death of Stalin, serious students of the USSR in the United States have tended to gravitate toward one of two distinct views of that country.

One view (Group A) sees the USSR as essentially just another Great Power, a rival of course, and one that is aggressive at times, but one that has an underlying set of values roughly equivalent to our own. This group believes that the USSR is really little more than the continuation of the old tsarist empire, with limited and generally legitimate aspirations: strategic survival, economic improvement, expansion of influence, acquisition (perhaps even monopoly) of markets, increased prestige.

Group A has traditionally included the more dovish of our foreign policy experts, those who have believed through the years that the USSR was maturing, that it would accept strategic parity with the United States as an adequate goal, and that meaningful negotiation with the USSR required only immense patience and the ability to understand and appreciate Russian strategic concerns. In the past there has been a measure of cool complacency in this view of our relations with the USSR.

The Group B view, on the other hand, has tended to accept at face value the implacable hostility of Soviet propaganda, most notably the ideological convictions that history has decreed a violent demise for capitalism at the hands of communism and that it is the duty of the

USSR to assist in that process. This group sees very little real distinction between the meaning of cold war, peaceful coexistence, and detente, with the first of these remaining the most accurate and expressive term. Regarding the possibility of Soviet acceptance of parity, Group B believes that Lenin decided the question long ago in just two words: *Kto - kogo*? ("Who (conquers) whom?"). There is no room for parity in such a formulation, and the Soviet determination to achieve superiority is a foregone conclusion. Group B tends to believe that Soviet aggressive intentions are immutable and have been restrained only by the limitations of Soviet capabilities.

In times of relative stability in U.S./USSR relations, the Group A view is traditionally the more acceptable, if for no other reason than that it is not alarmist. In past times of crisis, such as the Hungarian Revolution (1956), the Cuban missile crisis (1962), and the Soviet invasion of Czechoslovakia (1968), popular outrage swelled Group B ranks in the West temporarily, only to have them dissipate after a short time as the public returned to domestic concerns. As tensions relaxed, the Group A "defensive" interpretation of Soviet moves (to deny the evolution of Hungary and Czechoslovakia into platforms for hostile activity against the USSR, or in the case of Cuba, to achieve parity with the United States in the stationing of strategic weapons close to the adversary's territory) would gradually gain ground.

In the case of the 1979 invasion of Afghanistan, however, there was little room for complacency from either viewpoint.

In straight geopolitical (Group A) terms, the Soviet invasion is an aggressive, strategic thrust with apparently clear-cut military and economic objectives: closer Soviet proximity to the ever more vital Middle East oil supplies, a step toward attainment of a warm water port, an increased capability for intimidating all countries in the region (including China's friend, Pakistan), and a new link in the Soviet chain of containment being forged around China. As the first Soviet military conquest of territory outside its accepted sphere of influence since World War II, the invasion appears to have set a new precedent for aggression.

Paradoxically, from the Group B viewpoint, the Soviet move does have a defensive aspect. For Moscow it is impermissible, ideologically, for a socialist state to revert to a nonsocialist condition if it is within the power of the USSR to prevent it. Afghanistan, a new member of the so-called socialist family of nations after the 1978 coup, was clearly in the process of disintegrating under the attacks of Muslim insurgents in 1979. The rival ideology of Islam appeared to be on the point of overcoming Marxism-Leninism. Worse, this was in a country contiguous to those Soviet republics whose population is culturally and religiously far closer to Mecca than to Moscow.

If the insurgents had been allowed to succeed, the dangers of ideological infection spreading across the border into Central Asia would have been clear and immediate, even though there was no known organized anti-Soviet resistance there waiting to embrace the Afghan example. Even if the relative prosperity of the Soviet republics (compared to that of Afghanistan) had been enough to retain their loyalty to Moscow, the precedent of successful popular defiance to an accepted socialist regime could not have been permitted to stand. Too many other resistance-minded nationalities, inside the USSR itself as well as in other Warsaw Pact nations, might take heart from the Afghan example.

Another dispute frequently associated with the Group A/Group B controversy centers on the degree to which Moscow can (or even wishes to) control a foreign communist party. In absolute terms, of course, there is no such thing as complete control of one group of humans by another, and to that extent the argument is meaningless. There is, however, a considerable difference between norms of political argumentation, persuasion, and dissent that are acceptable in the West and the discipline of party obedience that is demanded of communists. This aspect is generally understood and accepted when speaking of conditions within any given party, but it is more debatable when speaking of inter-party relations.

Group A advocates tend to believe that the Communist Party of the Soviet Union (CPSU) can do little more than proffer friendly advice to "fraternal" parties, possibly augmented by private influence on particular individuals. They point to the success of various parties breaking away from Soviet control, whether those parties be in opposition (as in Spain), in power in an independent communist state (Yugoslavia), or even in power in a Warsaw Pact country (Romania). Because there is far less effective Soviet domination of foreign parties today than in the past, the implication is that this development is considered acceptable, perhaps even desirable, from the standpoint of Kremlin politics. The relationship between the CPSU and foreign parties is depicted as indeed fraternal, one of mutual (if sometimes guarded) trust, somewhat akin perhaps to the relations between the United States and its NATO allies. Group A would add that even if it were the Soviet desire to impose discipline and control, that goal would not lie within Soviet capabilities.

The Group B outlook on this question is again that the Soviet intent is for maximum control over foreign parties whenever an opportunity presents itself. This includes attempts to recruit foreign communists as direct agents of one of the Soviet intelligence services, with the twin goals of keeping the USSR informed on internal party maneuverings and of affecting local decisions in Moscow's interests. The Soviet effort to achieve maximum control is unremitting, and if their capability to do so has become weaker in recent years, that is less due to rejection of control as an end than rejection of terror as a means. The Soviet attitude is not fraternal—it is at least paternal, and it attempts to be patriarchal.

In analyzing Afghan developments, Group A tends to believe that until the Soviet invasion, events occurred largely without the knowledge, much less the interference, of the USSR. The 1965 formation and early activities of the People's Democratic Party of Afghanistan (PDPA), Daoud's 1973 coup, the 1977 reconciliation of the two antagonistic factions of the PDPA, and the plotting that led to Daoud's overthrow in 1978 are assumed to be purely domestic developments. Group A views the 1979 Soviet invasion as a disturbing aberration, perhaps the result of sudden, spontaneous outrage at the death of a Soviet deputy minister of interior in Afghanistan.

Group B, on the other hand, perceives a long-term pattern of Soviet aggressive intention in the country, modified by the pressures of other Soviet priorities and concerns, restrained by the limitations of Soviet capabilities, concealed by the fear of strong Western reaction should they become known, but consistent and openly emergent as soon as conditions permitted.

This book addresses that thesis.

Acknowledgments

It was at the suggestion of Dr. Richard F. Staar of the Hoover Institution that I embarked on this book. Without his encouragement and the steady flow of materials that he and his competent aide, Margit Grigory, sent me, it is doubtful that it would ever have seen the light of day.

My thanks also go to Hilja Kukk of the Hoover Library, whose pursuit of documentation on obscure facts and personages was relentless. The rest of the staff of the Hoover Library, along with that of the Social Sciences Library at the University of California at Berkeley, gave unstinting help, as did the librarians at the World Affairs Council in San Francisco. (Why can't the rest of the world be as helpful as librarians?)

Finally, for my wife Ruth, no words are enough. She collected and organized a large part of the material for this book, gave unflagging moral support, and suffered patiently through episodes of anger, all while managing a wildly fluctuating household of transient dependents.

None of the above, of course, bears any responsibility for errors of omission or commission that may have slipped into the work. Any such lapses are mine alone.

CHAPTER

1

The Historical Setting

The policy and practice of the Russian government has always been to push forward its encroachments as fast and as far as the apathy or want of firmness of other governments would allow it to go; but always to stop and retire when it was met with decided resistance and then to wait for the next favorable opportunity. . . .

(Lord Palmerston, British Foreign Secretary during the First Anglo-Afghan War, in an 1853 letter to Viceroy Clarendon.)[1]

Where the Indian subcontinent collides with Eurasia, the slow-motion conflict of geologic plates has given birth to the highest mountain chain in the world, the Himalayas. Astride their western end lies Afghanistan, the first opportunity in nearly two thousand miles for unimpaired travel north or south around the mountain barrier. It is a stark land of barren deserts and mountains, one-third the size of Mexico, and home today for about 15,000,000 Muslims, most of whom are engaged in subsistence agriculture.

In earlier centuries its strategic position led to alternate enrichment and devastation, as merchants and armies in turn marched through on their way to other lands. Later, a drying climatic trend, combined with the depredations of Genghis Khan and Tamerlane, caused traders to seek an alternative route to the Orient. The opening of the sea lanes in the sixteenth and seventeenth centuries largely destroyed Afghanistan's importance as a commercial crossroads. Its significance as a potential route for military invasion, however, remained unchanged.

In the nineteenth century, the British were keenly aware of tsarist Russia's expansion into Central Asia and of the eventual menace that such expansion might hold for India. Twice during that century the British invaded Afghanistan to forestall what they perceived as a Russian threat to take over the country and to use it as a staging area for an attack on India. Twice the Afghans made it so uncomfortable for them that, within a few years, the British withdrew. The Russians, witnessing this process and perhaps recalling that their own efforts to pacify mountain Muslims in the Caucasus had taken a full sixty-five years, prudently stayed away.

By the end of the century Russia and Britain had reached agreement: the British would control Afghanistan's foreign policy but would not occupy the country or try to manage its internal affairs; Russia formally conceded that Afghanistan lay outside its sphere of influence; and Afghanistan, perforce accepting British control over its foreign relations, dedicated itself to preserving its internal autonomy.

In 1900 Abdur Rahman Khan, the "Iron Amir," who ruled Afghanistan from 1880 to 1901, described his country's vulnerable position: "How can a small power like Afghanistan which is like a goat between two lions or a grain of wheat between two strong millstones of the grinding mill, stand in the way of the two stones without being ground to dust?"[2]

Even before putting the question, Abdur Rahman had found the answer. It was to keep Afghanistan from becoming a goat, a grain of wheat, or anything else remotely digestible by the hungriest of imperial lions or the most relentless of imperial millstones. His policies, like those of his predecessors and successors in Kabul's royal palace, were aimed at securing an internal toughness, impermeability, and integrity that would deter any foreign power from undertaking adventures on Afghan soil. At the same time he maintained a capability for smooth maneuvering between potential invaders, balancing one against the other. With these attributes, the Afghan tribes must have seemed to the two imperial millstones more like ballbearings than grains of wheat.

In the end, Russia and Britain came to understand that there were some advantages for all concerned in this situation—at least in the short run. Each had some fear of the other's intentions, and each perceived the useful role an independent country could play in keeping the two empires from coming into inadvertent conflict along a common border. Afghanistan became, in short, a model buffer state. So ideal was it for this role that in 1895 Britain and Russia agreed between them to add to it a new piece of territory, the Wakhan Corridor, running from the main body of Afghanistan to the Chinese border and dividing the North West Frontier Provinces of India from the Pamir Mountains in Russia. Abdur Rahman, who had to deal with some twenty major tribal insurrections within his own country during his twenty-one-year reign, had no desire to take on responsibility for this whole new set of independent potential insurgents, but he had little say in the matter.[3] He, better than anyone, understood the limitations that his country's economic backwardness had imposed on its independence in international affairs.

At the same time, that very backwardness was vital to continued Afghan internal self-determination. As long as the country remained poor and inaccessible, it would be unattractive to those with imperial designs.[4] The fastest way to build a modern military deterrent against foreign encroachment would be to develop the nation's economy with the aid of foreign investment, but to take that course would be to invite the enslavement it was designed to forestall.

To identify the problem was not to solve it; but in Abdur Rahman's view there was no question as to priorities: national independence took precedence over all other considerations, with unification of the warring tribes that made up the country taking a close second. Only after these two goals had been secured would he be willing to tolerate the foreign involvement necessary for economic development.

He was particularly adamant in his opposition to any kind of railroad construction in the country. Once a railroad was built, he noted, foreign troops could be called in at any time to protect foreign investments or, indeed, merely at the whim of any Great Power neighbor, and Afghanistan's primitive military forces would be helpless to stop them. Afghan independence would be the inevitable victim.[5] So trenchant were Abdur Rahman's arguments that to this day there are no railroads in Afghanistan; the last serious proposal to build one came in the mid-1970s, when a line from Kabul to the Iranian border was discussed as a possible link-up with the Iranian rail network. The project was to have been part of a $2 billion Iranian aid package that never did materialize.

With the death of Abdur Rahman in 1901 and the accession to the throne of his son, Habibullah, the former's rigid policies were relaxed to some degree. Habibullah had a lively curiosity, and among other innovations, he helped introduce the automobile, photography, and hydroelectric power to Afghanistan.[6] He also permitted far more domestic freedom than had his iron-willed father. Specifically, he permitted émigrés whom Abdur Rahman had exiled to return to Afghanistan and to become politically active.

Habibullah reigned in an age when pan-Islamism was spreading, and the phenomenon found reflection in his own court. There were three basic factions, all of them anti-British and pro-Turkish in their sympathies: (1) the conservative-clericals, who saw in Turkey a state that was grappling successfully with the necessary evil of modernization while still retaining Islam as the anchoring foundation; (2) the moderates, who viewed with favor Turkish modernization (especially the carefully paced nature of that modernization); and (3) the modernist-nationalists, the most anti-British, pro-Turkish of the three, who saw in the Turkish reforms changes that might be introduced in Afghanistan but at a much faster pace than in Turkey, once their feasibility had been demonstrated.[7] The modernist-nationalist newspaper, *Seraj al Akbar*, kept up a drum fire of anti-British propaganda that drew occasional royal reprimands when it overstepped what the amir felt were safe bounds.

Thus, with the outbreak of World War I, there was considerable pressure on Habibullah to join the Central Powers in their war with Britain and Russia. The amir, however, was well aware of both the geographic distance between Afghanistan and the Central Powers and the immediacy of his British and Russian borders. Consequently, despite agitation by the modernist-nationalists for a *jihad* (holy war) against the British, he maintained a careful neutrality throughout the war.[8] Habibullah was no Anglophile, but he had to reckon with the possibility of a joint Anglo-Russian attack on his country, and he could not afford to be at war with either one of those powers, let alone both at once. He was supported, if tepidly, in this realistic policy by some of the more influential moderates and conservative-clericals.

Even after one of the imperial threats had been removed by the disintegration of Russia into revolutionary chaos, Afghanistan remained neutral; the outcome of the war was beginning to become evident, and Habibullah prudently held to his previous policy.

In pursuing a course of relatively benevolent neutrality toward Britain, he was following in the footsteps of an illustrious forebear, Dost Mohammed, who refrained from helping Indian insurgents during the 1857 mutiny, despite heavy pressure from his countrymen to avenge the British victory over Afghanistan in the First Anglo-Afghan

War, some fifteen years before. As a prelude to that war, the British had annexed Peshawar and the surrounding territory that was inhabited by Pashtun tribes ethnically associated with the ruling Pashtuns of Afghanistan. Later, in 1893, the British were to fix their permanent Northwest Frontier Province (NWFP) border with Afghanistan along an arbitrary boundary called the Durand Line, which left the annexed territories permanently outside Afghan control.

Once World War I hostilities were over, Habibullah tried to capitalize on his restraint by asking the British to return voluntarily the Pashtun territories that they had annexed. Like Dost Mohammed before him, Habibullah met with a firm rebuff by the British, who also turned a deaf ear to his demands for Afghan independence in conducting its foreign affairs.

Shortly thereafter, on the first night of a hunting trip near Jalalabad in February 1919, Habibullah was killed by an assassin whose sponsor has never been clearly identified. It is not at all unlikely, however, that his son and successor, Amanullah, was connected in some way with his demise.

The evidence for such a conclusion is only circumstantial, but it is consistent. Amanullah had the twin motives of achieving power and, in line with his clearly modernist-nationalist sympathies, of removing power from a father whom he regarded as pro-British. The swiftness with which he reacted in taking power immediately on his father's death (neatly thwarting an uncle who tried to preempt the throne) bespeaks prior planning. The investigation of the assassination, which by all logic should have been pushed with great vigor, lasted just long enough to ensure that all of Amanullah's rivals remained in jail until he had secured firm control of the country. Those who survived this ordeal were then declared innocent and released, whereupon the investigation faded away.

In 1978 there appeared in the communist press hitherto unpublished material that adds even further weight to suspicions against Amanullah. In an article covering Habibullah's last months in power, it is stated that, shortly before Habibullah's assassination, one Taj Mohammed Paghman had fired a pistol at him and missed. Spared because of apparently perjured or confused testimony by two eyewitnesses, Taj Mohammed then wrote death-threat notes to Habibullah, to Habibullah's brother Inayatullah, to the foreign minister, and to the court chamberlain. The handwriting having been identified, Habibullah ordered the execution of Taj Mohammed and several accomplices, including a certain Abdur Rahman Ludin. That same night, however, Habibullah himself was assassinated. The death sentences of Taj Mohammed and the other earlier conspirators were quietly lifted. Only ten years later, after Amanullah himself had been deposed, did his successor have Ludin shot by a firing squad and Taj Mohammed blown from a cannon (the traditional Afghan punishment for especially serious crimes). Ludin and Taj Mohammed are cited in this 1978 communist account as having been "constitutionalists" who were very close to and "worked hand-in-glove with" Amanullah.[9]

Whether or not the circumstantial evidence against Amanullah reflects his direct responsibility for the assassination of his father, one must ask whether there was any foreign involvement in plotting the act. Two isolated pieces of information seem to support that thesis.

The first is a biographic note on Abdur Rahman Ludin (written, incidentally, by a different communist author from the one who described his complicity in the anti-Habibullah plot), in which he is described as ". . . a daring Leftist. . . . Especially after he returned from the Soviet Union, where he met Soviet leaders on Revolution Day, he used to praise the Soviets."[10] This trip to the USSR took place in November 1918, less than three months before Habibullah's assassination. While he was there, did Ludin discuss assassination plans with his Soviet contacts? Given the Soviet policy of world revolution at that time, it is difficult to imagine that he (or the Soviets for that matter) would have passed up the chance for such discussions, assuming that Habibullah's removal was already being contemplated by one side or the other.

The second piece of information is a curious statement made some years later by Fedor F. Raskolnikov, Lenin's envoy to Kabul during the early 1920s. Writing in the British journal *Labour Monthly* in 1929, Raskolnikov averred that Habibullah had failed "to take into consideration the changes which World War I and the October Revolution had brought about in the international position of Afghanistan. . . . After the October Revolution the Soviet Union was practically at war with Great Britain (but) Habibullah did not understand how to exploit these differences in favor of the national interests of his country and *for this incompetency he paid with his life*."[11] (Italics added.)

In other words, he was murdered for not waging a war that would be mutually advantageous to Afghanistan (to gain full independence from Britain) and to the USSR (to tie down the British forces, with which the USSR was "practically at war"). The fact of Afghan-Soviet collusion in Habibullah's murder may not be definitely established, but the motive and the instrument (Ludin) lend themselves to that interpretation.

CHAPTER
2

The First Twenty Years
1919–1939

The October Revolution not only changed fundamentally the fabric of domestic life in what had been tsarist Russia, but also involved the new Soviet state in a series of foreign confrontations. In Afghanistan during the same era, Amanullah's accession to the throne resulted in similar domestic upheaval and foreign complications, derivatives of his own experimentation in too-rapid reform at home and risky initiatives abroad. In the end, unlike Lenin and Stalin, Amanullah failed: Afghan traditional patterns proved too strong for his reformist ambitions, absolute ruler though he was. In the meantime, however, Afghan-Soviet relations developed in an intriguing blend of unacknowledged cooperation and hidden betrayal, much of which, even today, can only be inferred.

In late March 1919, just over a month after Habibullah's assassination, the government of Afghanistan received an official communication from the Soviet government, in which it was noted that the Russian Soviet Federated Socialist Republic (RSFSR) would be sending an envoy, one N. Bravin, to Afghanistan and Persia by way of Tashkent. The letter further noted that the RSFSR had annulled all treaties signed by the tsarist government with the rulers of that "global beast of prey," England.[1]

By May 14, when Amanullah's new foreign minister, Mahmud Tarzi, answered the Soviet letter, Afghanistan had attacked India and the Third Anglo-Afghan War was in full swing. In his reply, Tarzi wrote that he would welcome Bravin, but unfortunately the British were bombing Afghanistan "in answer to our establishing good relations with our neighbors." Tarzi also noted that Amanullah, on his first day on the throne, had annulled all of his predecessors' treaties with Britain and had declared Afghanistan's complete independence.[2]

In the meantime, Amanullah himself had written two warm letters to his "great and good friend," Lenin. In the first, dated April 7, he noted in straightforward prose that until then Afghanistan had not had the chance to maintain relations with other nations that "also favor freedom and equality." Inasmuch as Lenin himself had come out in favor of such principles, Amanullah was "happy to be the first to send a friendly word from the Afghan people."[3]

Amanullah's second letter to Lenin was written two weeks later, on April 21. There is no apparent reason for the communication, which appears to consist only of vague platitudes. Perhaps, in the meantime, there had been some other word from Lenin that provided concrete reference points Amanullah chose to answer in nonspecific terms. Among the more intriguing formulations is his reference to "mutual human relations for removing human poverty (being) a natural demand of mankind, especially in the present century, when the benefits of civilization, bringing happiness, call people to unification (sic— soyedineniye) and friendly mutual relations . . . first among two neighbors and then other peoples."[4] Leaving aside the possibility of hidden meanings in this message, its tone, like that of the earlier message, indicated that relations between Afghanistan and the RSFSR indeed commenced on a warm basis.

According to Raskolnikov, the Soviet Union was practically at war with Britain at the time of Habibullah's assassination. Within three months of that event, Afghanistan was actually at war with Britain—a war that Afghanistan itself had precipitated.

Not satisfied with waiting for a decisive British response to his declaration of independence, Amanullah sent his troops down through the Khyber Pass against the opposing British forces on the plains below. Though caught off balance, the British easily defeated the Afghans in the field. Having suffered losses in World War I, however, and with no desire for another debilitating occupation like those of the nineteenth century, the British accepted an Afghan bid for a truce and opened negotiations that eventually led to full independence for Afghanistan.

What led Amanullah to attack Britain, the most advanced military power of the age, a victor in the most destructive war in centuries, a country infinitely richer and stronger than his own? Was it merely an astute reading of the British mood? Or did he have reason to feel he could count on Soviet aid, if the British were to counterattack with an invasion of his kingdom? Was he perhaps counting on Soviet support for his claims to the NWFP and the regional capital of Peshawar? If so, he must have been disappointed, for the Soviets, hard-pressed in their own civil war, could offer no aid, and Amanullah had to accept reconfirmation of the Durand Line as the border between his country and India.

While there is no available record of any Soviet military commitment to Afghanistan in 1919, Amanullah may have been confident at least of Soviet financial backing. Since the days of Abdur Rahman, the British had provided an annual subsidy of more than one million rupees for the Afghan economy. By opening hostilities, Amanullah cut himself off from this support. A year after independence, however, in a treaty signed on September 13, 1920, in Kabul, the USSR obligated itself to supply one million gold rubles annually to the Afghans.[5] In addition, the USSR promised to deliver several aircraft, to provide five thousand rifles and ammunition for them, and to help Afghanistan in establishing an aviation school and a gunpowder plant. Agreement was also reached on sending Soviet technicians and other specialists to Afghanistan.[6] This treaty was not ratified until the following year and in fact was not honored in terms of actual payment until 1924.[7]

Whether or not the USSR specifically prompted the Afghans to undertake their war of independence, the conflict appeared to serve Moscow's interests. It occupied at least some of Britain's military energies and it inspired Indian revolutionaries and other restless colonial dissidents. With the communist optimism of 1919, some in the Kremlin may well have seen in Kabul's victory the harbinger of a whole series of revolts that would sweep through Asia, ending imperial Europe's domination of that continent.

In one respect this judgment was almost correct, but not in the manner foreseen by Moscow. The most enthusiastic opponents of European imperialism turned out to be not those southern and eastern Asians under British, French, or Dutch rule, but Russia's own Central Asian dependencies adjacent to Afghanistan.

Despite the initial warmth of Soviet-Afghan communications and the eventual aid, the beginnings of disagreement between them in Central Asia were visible from the outset of their relations. The March 27, 1919, letter announcing the dispatch of Bravin to Kabul, for example, was signed by one Bogoyavlenskiy, "People's Commissar of Foreign Affairs of the Turkestan Soviet Republic."

Afghan foreign minister Tarzi's reply, responding point by point in a most friendly fashion to everything written by Bogoyavlenskiy, was not sent to Bogoyavlenskiy at all but rather to Soviet Commissar of Foreign Affairs Georgiy Vasilyevich Chicherin in Moscow. Furthermore, in one cleverly worded sentence, Tarzi staked out an implicit Afghan claim to Turkestan, Bogoyavlenskiy's own purported nation.

"In accordance with a royal decree," he wrote, "the Governor General of Turkestan has been instructed to receive the Ambassador of the great government of Russia in the best manner . . . and to offer him cooperation and assistance in getting to Kabul. . . ."[8]

Tarzi neither identified the governor general, nor did he bother to specify whether the Afghan concept of Turkestan included all of the former Russian province under that name. In fact, there is no reason to believe that Kabul actually controlled any significant part of the province. History does not describe Moscow's initial reaction to this paper conquest, but within months Soviet concern began to be expressed privately. In September 1919, Leon Trotsky, Soviet commissar of war, wrote to the Central Committee of the Communist Party of the Soviet Union (CPSU) to warn against an English-sponsored confederation of Persia, Bukhara, Khiva, and Afghanistan, directed against Soviet Turkestan. Whether this was a real or imagined threat, Afghanistan was unquestionably active in helping the emir of Bukhara and the khan of Khiva (both of whom—like the amir of Afghanistan in his relations with the British before 1919—had enjoyed, under the tsars, sovereignty in internal but not in foreign affairs) to defend themselves against the Red Army and to suppress indigenous revolutionaries.[9]

What the Afghans had in mind was the formation of a Central Asian Confederation, with Kabul the dominant power. Such a confederation would have provided an excellent buffer against Russian encroachments from the north, as well as furthering Afghanistan's own pan-Islamic aspirations. As a start, Amanullah opened diplomatic relations with Bukhara and Khiva in order to afford them legal recognition as sovereign states. He hoped, ultimately, to do the same with Turkestan, and to include all of them in his projected confederation.[10]

For the Russian communists, however, the expansion of feudal Afghanistan at the expense of socialist Russia was a historical anachronism: it contradicted not only the proper, programmed course of history as dictated by Marx, but Russian state self-interest as well. The latter half of 1919, however, was a time of serious difficulty for the USSR, as White forces in Russia marched north along the Don River as far as Voronezh, and Moscow itself seemed to be threatened. Whatever the USSR's Central Asian intentions, Soviet capabilities were being critically strained closer to home. It is perhaps for that reason that in November 1919, shortly after Trotsky's warning, Lenin wrote to Amanullah, "Afghanistan is the only independent Muslim state in the world, and fate sends the Afghan people the great historic task of uniting about itself all enslaved Mohammedan peoples and leading them on the road to independence."[11]

If there was any sincerity in these words at all, it lay in Moscow's hope that Afghan pan-Islamic aspirations would find outlets to the east, west, or south—anywhere, in fact, but to the north. It was a vain hope. Afghanistan worked hard to prop up the shaky Bukharan emir and the Khivan khan, and once the Red Army had deposed them (in September 1920), gave them sanctuary and a base from which to operate their governments in exile. Worse, the Afghans gave direct, discreet aid to t¹e Basmachi, partisans who continued to resist Soviet control in the region.

Soviet sources define *Basmach* as "member of a counter-revolutionary band in Central Asia in the period of the struggle to establish Soviet power,"[12] and as deriving from the Turkic word *basmak*, meaning "to fall on, attack."[13] A French scholar asserts that it means "go barefoot" (*va-nu-pieds*),[14] which, whether accurate or not, is evocative of the Basmachi's true status. For they were fundamentally partisans whose common denominator was inferiority in overall numbers and armaments to the Red Army forces they confronted.

Despite the paucity of literature in English on the Basmachi, they are worth closer attention, not so much for their effect on Soviet-Afghan relations (though they were a pivotal factor) as for the striking parallels they provide with today's Afghan insurgent movements. Indeed, it almost seems that the basic difference is only one of area, with the locale having moved south: Afghanistan today is the equivalent of the Central Asian battlefields of yesteryear, while Pakistan is repeating Afghanistan's uneasy former role as a safe haven and undeclared source of support for the insurgency. (Compared with Afghanistan in the 1920s, however, Pakistan is forced to be far more discreet in any aid it might wish to give the rebel cause; the relative strength and proximity of the USSR is far greater.)

Two aspects of the Basmachi movement deserve particular notice. First, it was durable. Regular armed clashes with the Red Army went on for at least fifteen years, from 1917 to 1932, and often involved significant numbers of troops on both sides. For example, Soviet sources (who have no reason to emphasize Basmachi strength) put Basmachi numbers in the Fergana valley alone at thirty thousand during the summer of 1920.[15]

Second, there is a consistent record of betrayal of the Soviet cause by Moscow's own protégés on the spot, and an equally consistent Basmachi record of success in commanding loyalty among the local population, despite the overwhelming odds against them. Corollary to this was the bewildering facility of the lesser Basmachi leaders and their followers to make apparent capitulation to the Red Army, to volunteer service with it, and then to betray it at the first opportune moment.[16]

For some reason, despite Soviet recognition of this pattern and the resultant general order that all capitulating Basmachi be disarmed, dispersed, and held under close control, the Soviets kept falling into the same trap. The Basmachi were such good fighters and so familiar with the terrain that the temptation to use them was irresistible. (In 1980 there were reports of a similar program: Afghan tribesmen from one section of the country were allegedly being hired at ten times the normal soldier's daily wage to fight insurgents in other parts.[17] It is not clear whether such forces were working directly with Soviet troops or alongside regular Afghan units. Either way, frictions, betrayals, and mutinies would seem to be the inevitable result.)

Perhaps the most famous of the Basmachi "traitors" was Enver Pasha, who had been the young war minister of the Ottoman empire during World War I. Having been ousted from that position following defeat of the Central Powers, he went first to Germany and then on to Moscow, where he became known as a nationalist Bolshevik. He persuaded Soviet authorities that he could rally the Central Asian Muslims into an anti-British *jihad*, and using Afghanistan as a base, drive the English from India. With Soviet backing he went off to Bukhara but in November 1921, under cover of a hunting trip, he defected to the Basmachi. In early 1922 he helped rally and unite various Basmachi bands, swiftly building an army of some twenty thousand. And on May 19, 1922, as chief of the "Turkish Central Asian Republic," he sent a note to the Russian Socialist Federated Soviet Republic (RSFSR) demanding recall of all Red Army troops then stationed in Khiva, Bukhara, and Turkestan.[18]

Although Enver Pasha was the most famous, he was by no means the only such defector from the Soviet ranks. The Red Army had taken Bukhara on September 3, 1920,[19] and had set up the appropriate party and state organizations, staffing their upper levels with ideologically "correct" leaders. It was doubtless this apparent control that permitted the USSR, some eleven days later, to agree solemnly by treaty in Kabul that Bukhara and Khiva would be granted complete self-determination.[20] The Afghans, who had insisted on this proviso as one way of gaining prestige with fellow Muslims, were perhaps unaware of the reason for the sudden Soviet acquiescence. Probably by the time their own communications could inform them of the Soviet takeover of the two states, the treaty already had been signed—though not ratified.

Through the next year the Soviet leadership in Bukhara apparently behaved as obediently as Moscow expected. The Afghans, possibly feeling that they had been double-crossed, did not ratify the treaty until August 1921.[21] When they did, it may have been because in this specific instance their information was better than that of the Soviets. It was in that same August that the chief of the Central Executive Committee of the Bukharan People's Soviet Republic, Usman Khodzha Pulatkhodzhayev, turned over to the Basmachi twelve Red Army collaborators, six of whom were summarily executed.[22]

If the Afghans appeared to know of this act and recognize its significance, Moscow clearly was unaware of it; Pulatkhodzhayev remained in power until December 1921 when, in an attempt to disarm by trickery and then to arrest the Red Army garrison at Dushanbe, his true pro-Basmachi allegiance emerged.[23] In the aftermath of this failed effort, the extent of anti-Soviet sentiment among the Bukharan leadership suddenly became clear. How many actually went over to the Basmachi is unrecorded, but they included the commissar of war and his deputy, the chief of police (militia), and even the chief of the secret police (Cheka)![24] (It is an irony of history that the Uzbek Fayzullah Khodzhayev, the only prominent Central Asian leader to remain unshakeably loyal to Moscow through these turbulent years, was to be executed by Stalin in the 1937 purges—as a bourgeois nationalist![25])

In fact, it was not a question of these individuals being defectors, any more than the Hungarian leadership under Imre Nagy or the Czech leadership under Alexander Dubcek were defectors. In all three cases, the population supported the so-called renegades in their bid for independence, and it was only the appearance on the scene of an overwhelming alien military force that restored Moscow's control. Even the language used by Soviet propaganda in Central Asia served as a precursor of what was to be repeated three and four decades later in Europe—and nearly sixty years later in Afghanistan. As expressed in a session of the Bukhara soviet in August 1922, after more obedient leaders had filled the seats vacated by Pulatkhodzhayev and the others, "The Russian Red Army came to Bukhara not on its own initiative, for the sake of achieving some mercenary goal, but, on the contrary, at the request of the Bukharan People's Soviet Republic, to liberate its territory and downtrodden people from the ongoing Basmachi Movement. . . ."[26]

Soviet actions in Central Asia during this period resulted in popular reactions in Afghanistan itself. In 1919, the Bravin mission lost two, killed, and eighteen, wounded, in one armed attack. In 1922, five members of the Soviet Embassy were killed in Kabul, an unsuccessful attempt was made on the lives of the consul general and other members of his mission in Herat, and several couriers were murdered. A Soviet source ascribes these attacks to the actions of British agents, but without any evidence to support the charge.[27] It is more likely that at least the 1922 attacks were by displaced Basmachi or by Basmachi sympathizers.

Afghan popular opinion in favor of the Basmachi was a key factor in permitting that movement to remain viable for another decade despite Red Army efforts to stamp it out. Afghan sympathy permitted Basmachi bands to cross at will over a border too difficult for the Red Army to patrol effectively, and this was an important factor in their survival. Soviet sources accuse world imperialism of having supplied significant material support to the Basmachi, but the evidence they produce to substantiate this charge indicates a low level of quantity and quality of foreign aid (e.g., occasional interceptions of camel trains with some rifles and ammunition).[28]

Although the USSR did eventually quell the movement, the nationalism that lay at its roots is an innate (if occasionally dormant) aspect of any particular culture dominated by another. Indeed, with the example that the Afghan insurgency is providing today, it is not impossible that violent manifestations of nationalism will recur in Soviet Central Asia in the not-too-distant future.

The Basmachi movement was to reach a peak in 1922 just before Enver Pasha's death in action (he commanded twenty thousand troops at the time, besides having the allegiance of the former Soviet leadership in Bukhara).[29] By then, however, a series of diplomatic moves was already paving the way for firmer Soviet control over the territory north of Afghanistan.

The Afghan-Soviet treaty signed in 1920 and ratified by Kabul in 1921 contained, in addition to its articles on the various Soviet assistance measures and Khivan/Bukharan "self-determination," provisions for establishing Soviet consulates in five Afghan towns and for reciprocal Afghan privileges in the USSR.[30] This Soviet consular representation was far in excess of any justifiable need, at least as far as normal diplomatic transactions were concerned, and was looked upon with understandable skepticism by the British.

Perhaps as a result of this skepticism, the preamble to the Anglo-Soviet trade agreement signed in March 1921 included a Soviet obligation to refrain from any military or propaganda moves that might affect British interests in India or Afghanistan. This appeared to hold up a Soviet project for dispatching Indian revolutionaries via Afghanistan to India.[31] It did not, however, put a stop to similar activities already under way, and in 1923 the British forced the recall of the Soviet ambassador in Kabul, threatening an economic boycott in retaliation for his aid to Pashtun rebels in the NWFP.[32]

Finally, in November 1921 the Afghans and the British signed their own agreement, containing among other provisions an Afghan pledge not to permit establishment of Soviet consulates in eastern Afghanistan.[33]

Until this time, Amanullah had been experimenting rather freely in international intrigue. Not only had he lent support to the Basmachi in Soviet Central Asia, but (at least according to Soviet sources) he had closed an eye to British activities in the same field. At the same time, with traditional Afghan evenhandedness in such matters, he had not objected in principle to the passage of men and arms from the Soviet Union through Afghanistan on their way to stir up trouble in India, though he did insist that the two proceed separately, the arms to be under strict Afghan control during passage.[34]

He was, however, under increasingly heavy economic pressure, the Soviet subsidy at this time still being only a promise and his own internal reforms being more expensive than anticipated. Not only were they expensive financially, but they began to incur some unpleasant political costs as well. In 1925 a revolt against his rule broke out in Khost, and it was only put down thanks to the use of German and Soviet pilots flying missions against the rebels.[35]

That same year Soviet forces occupied a small island in the Amu Darya River (known as Urta Taigal or Yangi Qala), on the border with Afghanistan. The Afghans protested, and as a result of the findings of a joint Afghan-Soviet border commission, Afghan possession of the island was confirmed.[36]

It was probably a combination of Soviet "fraternal assistance" against Amanullah's internal enemies and the peaceful acceptance of the border commission's findings that resulted the following year in an outwardly more cordial Soviet-Afghan treaty, one that seemed to rule out any further Afghan support to the Basmachi.[37] In fact, however, there was very little change; the Afghans were to plead, and the Soviets to agree, that there was little of a practical nature the Afghans could do to deny their territory to the Basmachi.[38]

At the same time, the Afghan tilt toward the USSR may also have been partially responsible for a greater Soviet aggressiveness in 1926–27 as they tried to stir up trouble in British-controlled Baluchistan, to the south of Afghanistan. Like the previous attempt among the Pashtuns, however, the attempt was frustrated by British threats of economic retaliation.[39]

While backing away from these efforts at subverting India, the USSR continued to increase its influence inside Afghanistan: the thirteen Soviet aircraft that had helped to put down the Khost revolt remained as a gift to the Afghans, along with the loan of thirty pilots to operate them; Soviet engineers began work on a road to connect Kabul to the northern provinces; and Soviet nationals began to appear ever more frequently in Afghan government offices.[40] In small measure the

USSR was attempting then what it was to repeat on a much grander scale thirty years later.

Meantime, however, the world was moving toward the pivotal year 1929, memorable in the West for the onset of the Great Depression, in the USSR for industrialization/collectivization, and in Afghanistan for the temporary dispossession of the monarchy by a Tadzhik bandit, Bacha-e-Saqao ("waterboy's son").

The fall of Amanullah in Afghanistan was the direct result of his unpopular reforms. Among other gestures disruptive of the status quo, Amanullah decreed that Afghan males should wear Western dress when in Kabul. He also demanded land reform, women's education, and abolition of the veil for women. These reforms, supposed to set the country on the road to modernization, produced a backlash of surprising ferocity that led instead to a temporary breakup of the Afghan state. The tribes rose up in rebellion, warring first against Amanullah and then—as has been traditional throughout Afghan history when central power has been eliminated—against each other. Bacha-e-Saqao took over Kabul and with it the ostensible reins of power. He did it, however, with a robber band that was no substitute for the semiprofessional Afghan army and with a set of "ministers" most of whom were illiterate. He lasted for nine months, being overthrown and executed by Nader Shah in late 1929.

Nader Shah had returned to Afghanistan with tacit British aid, accompanied by his two brothers and raising an army of Pashtuns as he passed through the NWFP. (He was specifically enjoined from doing this by the British, perhaps because they thought he might overlook the opportunity if they did not remind him of it; there was no doubt in anyone's mind that the only sensible way to go about restoring a responsible monarch to the throne was by application of adequate military force.)

Before Nader Shah and his brothers fought the decisive battles that disposed of Bacha-e-Saqao, a similar incursion from the north under Soviet auspices had met with failure. Ghulam Nabi, Afghan ambassador to Moscow, appeared on the Soviet-Afghan border at Termez with some eight hundred "Afghan volunteers" who inexplicably materialized on Soviet territory with machine guns, artillery, and even air support. His purpose, said Ghulam Nabi, was to restore Amanullah to the throne. To aid Ghulam Nabi in managing his "Afghan" forces came a Russian, one Primakov, a former Soviet military attaché in Kabul.

After some initial successes, including the conquest of Mazar-e-Sharif and the recruitment of a motley (but now truly Afghan) troop of volunteers to augment his Soviet contingent, Ghulam Nabi withdrew to the north: he had learned that Amanullah, then in Kandahar and sensing the dissolution of his remaining support in the country, had decided to remove himself to India and to give up the fight.[41]

It had been a curious invasion for several reasons. The concept was probably to have Ghulam Nabi march on Kabul at the head of the same army whose hard corps was Primakov's disciplined, thinly disguised Soviet unit. After restoring Amanullah, Ghulam Nabi would have been the power behind the throne, while Primakov (presumably) would have been the power behind Ghulam Nabi. At that point, the USSR would have had an excellent opportunity to influence if not largely to control the Afghan government.

One might have anticipated that Ghulam Nabi, on hearing of Amanullah's capitulation, would have sent him an urgent appeal to hold fast (or even to come join his northern forces), in anticipation of the final, triumphant drive to the capital. Even if there had been temporary setbacks at the hands of Bacha-e-Saqao's ragged army, surely the infusion of a few more Soviet troops, properly disguised as Afghans, would have turned the tide . . .

Ghulam Nabi made no such appeal and quietly went into temporary exile in the USSR. Nader Shah then seized the initiative, and although the British did not supply their own military commanders to help him, the new Afghan ruler's implicit debt of gratitude was, if anything, to England, not to the USSR.

At first glance, the support the USSR gave Amanullah (however reformist his intentions) seems out of character. Indeed, it must have been an ideologically painful decision for the Soviet leadership to make. Bacha-e-Saqao was a charismatic peasant leader, Amanullah a hereditary feudal monarch. Soviet support for the latter was difficult to explain to the foreign idealists who made up so much of the USSR's support abroad. Furthermore, from a practical standpoint Bacha-e-Saqao was already in power and would have been much easier for the USSR to champion than to overthrow. Finally, when the USSR did opt for support of Amanullah it did so in such a hesitant, ineffective way that it lost more than it would have if it had done nothing at all. Why did it move in the direction it did, and why with such uncharacteristic indecisiveness?

As to direction, it may be that the USSR detected in the charismatic Tadzhik peasant a much greater potential menace to its own restless Central Asian republics than the Pashtun king, Amanullah. The former had direct ethnic ties with the rebellious Tadzhiks who made up so much of the Basmachi movement and could be expected to expand his influence northward. Fresh in the Russian memory were the betrayals of the entire Bukharan Soviet leadership when Moscow had tried to exert control before. There was, if anything, less reason for the USSR to put its trust in self-made Bacha-e-Saqao than it had Pulatkhodzhayev, its own protégé. By contrast, Amanullah's interests and ties lay in the equally restless Pashtun tribes that were causing the British such problems in the NWFP.

The hesitancy of the Soviet approach was probably caused by Moscow's dawning perception of a domestic problem: the massive peasant discontent with agricultural collectivization throughout the USSR. Peasant resistance was solidifying everywhere and was accompanied in Central Asia by a sudden resurgence of the Basmachi phenomenon.[42] This was no time for Soviet commitments to be extended or for Soviet armed forces to be occupied anywhere but in the homeland, where they were needed to suppress internal unrest.

For his part, Nader Shah, correctly gauging his countrymen's implacable hostility to the reforms imposed by Amanullah, backed quickly away from the most radical of them. The fragility of the Afghan nation-state had been clearly illustrated by its fragmentation when Amanullah was deposed, and Nader Shah had as his first order of business the reunification and proper internal administration of his country. To accomplish this, he needed to reduce to a minimum the distractions of foreign affairs and to ensure tranquility on his borders.

In 1931 he signed a new pact with the USSR, one that reiterated and strengthened Amanullah's 1926 commitments against the use of Afghan territory as a base for subversive activities aimed against the USSR (i.e., a safe haven for the Basmachi). Unlike Amanullah, he enforced it. Under the combined blows of the Red Army in Central Asia and the suddenly effective Afghan border patrols, Basmachi activities began to wither. In early 1931, Afghan forces drove Ibrahim Beg, the most durable of the Basmachi leaders, back over the border into the USSR, where he was finally betrayed by a Central Asian tribesman, taken into custody by Soviet forces, and executed after a show trial. By the end of 1933 the last reported cohesive Basmachi band had crossed back into Iran from a brief transborder raid,[43] but to all intents and purposes, Basmachi operations with ties to Afghanistan had ceased by the end of 1931.

At the same time, Nader Shah tried to put a stop to anti-British revolutionary activity based in Afghanistan. This effort was exemplified by the Red Shirt Movement, a professedly Leninist Pashtun group that was alternately in and out of favor with Moscow and that tried to stir up trouble in the NWFP. It had enjoyed some covert moral support from Amanullah, but Nader Shah discouraged its activities as much as possible.

Of the two Afghan rulers, Amanullah and Nader Shah, the latter was undoubtedly more effective in permitting the USSR finally to stabilize its uncertain position in Central Asia. Yet to this day, even as it excoriates Nader Shah as a British puppet, Soviet literature regrets the passing of Amanullah from the Afghan political scene. Although Amanullah was progressive in his internal policies, in practical terms he provided more problems to the USSR than did Nader Shah, who was scrupulous in his adherence to traditional Afghan policies of non-alignment and neutrality.

Two particular "anti-Soviet" actions may lie at the root of Soviet displeasure with Nader Shah.

The first was his sweeping dismissal of the Soviet advisors, pilots, and engineers whom Amanullah had invited to help manage the country, while at the same time, he denied a Soviet request for establishment of a commercial mission in Afghanistan. In place of the departing Soviet advisors, he hired Germans, Italians, Japanese, and Indians (but not British).[44] Following the isolationist precepts of Abdur Rahman, Nader Shah wanted as foreign advisors only those who were unlikely to be supported by neighboring armed forces in case of any disagreements.

The second action was his forthright disposal of that Soviet favorite Ghulam Nabi, who by this time had returned to Kabul from his Central Asian exile. Ghulam Nabi's outspoken support for Amanullah did not earn him many friends in the new Nader Shah regime, which also must have looked askance at his former Soviet ties. Eventually, in the fall of 1932, Nader Shah suggested that Ghulam Nabi leave Afghanistan permanently—though with a royal pension on which to maintain himself in appropriate comfort. While pretending to think this over, Ghulam Nabi allegedly started fomenting rebellion "in the southern province," presumably in the restless regions along the Durand Line.[45]

Summoned before Nader Shah in November 1932, he answered the charges against him in an insulting manner and was executed forthwith. (The trial whose verdict condemned him was actually held post mortem.) While there is no proof that the USSR was directly involved in Ghulam Nabi's purported subversive activities on this occasion, his previous involvement with Primakov and the Soviet irregulars leads to the suspicion that he was not working alone. The south of Afghanistan, then as now, has been an area of considerable Soviet interest, and active Soviet preparations for supporting tribal uprisings in Baluchistan had been proceeding for some time.[46] Furthermore, his boldness in insulting his monarch, an impropriety that turned out to be fatal, may have stemmed from a belief on his part that he had Soviet backing.[47]

His execution ushered in a brief era of political violence that was not to be matched until the communist coup of 1978, nearly fifty years later. In the space of precisely one year, there were five victims in three separate assassination incidents: three members of the British Embassy staff in Kabul, the Afghan ambassador to Berlin (a brother of the king), and finally, on the first anniversary of Ghulam Nabi's execution, King Nader Shah himself. In each case the assassin was a student who was studying or had studied at the German School (Nejat) in Kabul.

The organization that promoted these assassinations was called the Young Afghans, and claimed to be the direct heir to an earlier organization of the same name whose goal had been the formation of a constitutional government. These latter-day Young Afghans, however, declared that their aim was the "subversion of the existing government and of its basis, the Islamic code," justifying their revolutionary position on an alleged secret British manipulation of the Afghan government.[48] (This allegation was certainly untrue, but became a consistent major motif in Soviet propaganda on Afghanistan starting in the 1930s.)

The focus of the Young Afghan agitation in Afghanistan was the Nejat; abroad, it was the Afghan student community in Germany. An important link between these two groups was Mrs. Mehta (Mitha) Singh, the German wife of "a revolutionary Sikh of the Ghadr Party, who, with Moscow's assistance, had taken up residence in Kabul to plot against British rule in India."[49] The Shahi Bazaar Coffee House, which she owned and operated, was a regular meeting place for students from the Nejat school. Mehta Singh himself had acted as a communications link between the students in Kabul and the last surviving member of Ghulam Nabi's family in Germany.[50] Thus, via the Singhs the USSR must have been fully aware of the activities of the Young Afghans if, indeed, they were not directly influencing them. The Singhs themselves were closely acquainted with Nader Shah's assassin.[51]

From the standpoint of the Afghan students, however, motivation for the assassinations was probably a blend of local politics and personal revenge. Marxist–Leninist ideology per se does not appear to have played any detectable role, and with the death of Nader Shah the violence abated.

Nader Shah's son and successor, the young Zahir Shah, "reigned but did not rule" for the next thirty years. In the Afghan tradition, his uncles ran the country in his name. A kindly, gentle man, Zahir Shah remained on the throne for four decades until he was finally deposed by his forceful first cousin, Mohammed Daoud, in 1973.

For the rest of the 1930s and on into the middle of the 1940s, Afghan-Soviet relations were unremarkable. For the Afghans it was a period of rest and quiet progress, interrupted by some tribal difficulties and other growing pains. For the Soviet Union it was a time of gigantic turmoil: collectivization, famine, the purges, and finally World War II. It is probably thanks to these overriding preoccupations that the USSR backed away from pursuit of more aggressive policies in Afghanistan during this period.

CHAPTER

3

World War II and Its Aftermath

1940–1953

By the middle of 1940, the initial stages of World War II in Europe and the protracted Sino-Japanese War in the Orient appeared to offer implicit sanction for forcible rearrangement of international borders. Following his successful incorporation of the Sudetenland into the Third Reich, Hitler had signed with the USSR a nonagression treaty that permitted the latter to occupy the Baltic States, Moldavia, eastern Poland, and parts of Finland. Soviet appreciation of these opportunities was expressed not only in propaganda support for Germany against British imperialism, but more concretely, in trade that supplied food and raw materials to the German economy.

Meanwhile, the Wehrmacht had overrun all opposition on the mainland of Europe, and Britain was the last remaining major opponent confronting Hitler. Virtually all of England's energies were focused on defense of the home island against the cross-channel invasion that seemed imminent.

All of these factors (not least the apparently pro-German bias of the USSR) created a potential opportunity for Afghanistan to reconquer the historically Afghan lands in the NWFP that had been occupied by the British for the last century. Adding to the temptation was an explicit German promise to guarantee Afghan borders up to the limits of the eighteenth-century Afghan Durrani Empire (including all of the NWFP and more), as well as the port of Karachi. In return the

Germans asked that the Afghans foment unrest along India's northwest frontiers.[1]

Twice in the past century the Afghans had been given similar opportunities to reconquer their land. In 1857 the Indian Mutiny had all but driven Britain from the subcontinent (and with Afghan help might indeed have succeeded in so doing); and in 1914–18, the participation of Turkey as a cobelligerent of Germany in World War I had led to efforts to enlist Afghanistan in a *jihad* against Britain. In both of these cases Afghanistan remained true to its treaty obligations with Britain and stayed neutral.

History repeated itself again. On August 17, 1940, at a time when Britain's fortunes in the war were at their lowest ebb, Zahir Shah proclaimed Afghan neutrality.

A year later, the Nazi attack on the USSR had changed the USSR from a tacit Axis ally into a blood enemy, and Afghanistan found itself surrounded on three sides by Allied cobelligerents (China, the USSR, and British India) and on the fourth by Allied-dominated Iran. In August 1941, though both Britain and the USSR were still on the defensive and very hard pressed by the Axis, they had acted jointly to eliminate an effort to enlist Iran on the Axis side. Had the Axis effort been successful, it would have secured Iranian oil for Germany and sealed off the USSR's southern flank as a supply route from the West.

Instead, however, on August 25 the USSR and Britain sent forces into Iran and conquered the country, encountering and overcoming only light opposition from the Iranian army and navy. On October 9 and 11, they followed up this military success with diplomatic pressure on Kabul to remove all nondiplomatic Axis personnel from Afghanistan. The charge was that German agitators were fomenting trouble among the Pashtun tribes and causing casualties to loyal native troops along the Indian frontier. These accusations were similar to those made by the British to the Iranian authorities just before the Anglo-Soviet incursion there, and the threat of similar actions against Afghanistan was apparent in Kabul.[2]

The Afghans delayed briefly (by calling for a tribal assembly, [*loyah jirgah*] to decide the issue) in honor of the Pashtun code of ethics that obliges a host to provide sanctuary for any guest. In the end they capitulated to Allied pressure, but in an effort to be even-handed decreed that *all* nondiplomatic persons who were citizens of any of the belligerent powers would have to leave. Furthermore, before pro-

ceeding with the deportations, they secured British promises of safe
conduct for Axis nationals while they were transiting India en route
home. (The British only partially honored this pledge, interning some
of the Germans whom they specifically suspected of having carried out
subversive activities. The Afghans, though angered by this violation of
a solemn commitment, could do nothing in retaliation.)

As World War II widened to include Japan and the United States,
Afghanistan began to feel the effects of the conflict on its economy. On
the one hand it could sell to the Allies at war-inflated prices all of the
surplus foodstuffs it could produce—and move to market. As a result,
foreign monetary reserves built up rapidly, especially because there
were few goods available to buy from the belligerents.

On the other hand, the war completely disrupted those important
aspects of the Afghan economy that depended on normal foreign trade
patterns. The single largest source of foreign revenues before the war
had been the profitable London market for karakul skins. Wartime
London had no use for such luxury items, and the beginnings of an
American market (which was to develop significantly in the late 1940s)
also fell off sharply when the United States became a belligerent in
December 1941. The Axis markets were at a complete standstill during
the entire war and for some time thereafter.[3]

Another problem caused by the war was the difficulty in replacing
manufactured products, especially machinery needed for agriculture,
irrigation, food processing, and transportation. The prewar foreign
producers of these items were manufacturing armaments, and Afghanistan could not make its own substitutes. Thus the boom in wartime
agricultural sales was limited by the inability of the Afghan farmers to
bring new land into production, to exploit existing cultivated acreage
to the fullest, or to transport harvests to the international markets.[4]

With the end of hostilities, the leadership looked for ways to improve the economy by using its wartime accumulation of foreign exchange. In 1946 it turned to the Morrison-Knudsen Company of Boise,
Idaho, for repair and restoration of four irrigation dams, the construction of new irrigation canals, and the rebuilding of 450 kilometers of
highway, all in the Helmand Valley, west of Kandahar. The initial
contract was for $17 million, which the Afghan treasury was well able to
absorb without outside assistance.[5]

As one of the pioneer postwar American efforts to aid an underdeveloped country, the Helmand project suffered from many of the

problems and embarrassments that usually beset such efforts: bad cost estimates, cultural conflicts, broken promises, bureaucratic delays, and the like. It is beyond the scope of this work to discuss these in detail. Suffice it to say that the American involvement and presence in the Helmand was to continue for over three decades, and was to be removed only in late 1978, when insurgency against the newly installed communist government put the lives of Americans there in jeopardy. Its very durability thus bespeaks a considerable measure of success, despite the early difficulties and the complicating political problems discussed in the text.

Cost overruns soon raised the Helmand project estimate to $40 million, and the Afghans were forced to turn to external financing sources. Loans by the Import-Export Bank amounted to $21 million in 1949 and $18.5 million in 1954; by 1956 Morrison-Knudsen had spent $54 million on the project, and the United States government had become involved as a direct funder of part of the project through the International Cooperation Administration. The loans that the Afghans were able to secure were far smaller than they wished, and the work went forward slowly.[6]

The transition of the project from one that involved a simple contract with a single foreign firm, to one that required funding by a foreign bank, to one that relied on grants from a foreign government was an unforeseen development. So was the length of time that was to elapse before any positive benefits were obtained. This was in contrast with the Soviet aid projects of the 1950s that gave relatively quick, visible results.[7]

Meanwhile, however, a political problem of long standing became more acute and overshadowed all other foreign policy considerations for Afghanistan. In 1947, with the breakup of British India into the newly independent states of India and Pakistan, the Afghans saw perhaps their last chance to retrieve by negotiation their lost territories in the NWFP. Once the British had departed from the territories, the Afghans would no longer be able to negotiate with those who had originally annexed the disputed area. Pakistan's own rebuff to any Afghan overtures to take back the land was a foregone conclusion. As in previous eras, however, the Afghans were soon disabused of any hopes that the British would reward Afghan restraint in World War II with territorial concessions.

The border (Durand Line) had been established in 1893, when

Indian foreign secretary Sir Mortimer Durand led a delegation to Kabul for talks with Abdur Rahman. The latter had appeared to welcome the fixing of a boundary (even if it did not satisfy Afghan claims) in order to halt what he perceived as relentless British encroachments on his territory. Reference points were agreed upon, with the actual boundary to be determined by survey teams on the spot. These teams were concerned primarily with military offense and defense, but they were supposed also to preserve tribal integrity insofar as possible. Even if the teams had been scrupulously conscientious (which they apparently were not), the Durand Line would have divided an ethnically homogeneous population.

It was particularly galling to Kabul that the 1947 British-run plebiscite in the NWFP to determine which state would have jurisdiction there offered only two choices: India or Pakistan. In Afghan eyes, the choices at least should have included self-determination, if not outright union with Afghanistan. Although 99 percent of those who voted opted for union with Pakistan, only 55.5 percent of the enfranchised electorate turned out to vote. Three political parties championing independence and claiming to represent nearly 50 percent of the electorate ordered their adherents to boycott the plebiscite, on grounds that the choices were not broad enough.[8] The relatively weak voter turnout indicates that their call was heeded by at least some of the electorate, though many other factors also would have tended to limit the size of the vote in such primitive, rugged territory.

It was this Afghan frustration in pressing their territorial claims that led them to invent the new state of Pashtunistan, comprising not only the NWFP but also the southwest deserts occupied by Baluchi tribesmen. Afghan propaganda endowed this purported nation with a political and social unity that it did not in fact possess: though linguistically and ethnically akin, the various tribes inhabiting Pashtunistan were customarily at war with one another and only occasionally found partial unity when resisting efforts by outsiders to impose foreign control. (It must be noted that the same independent spirit manifests itself on the Afghan side of the border as well: traditionally, rule from Kabul has been no more acceptable to the mountain tribes than rule from Islamabad.)

As a further sign of its displeasure, Afghanistan cast the only vote in the UN General Assembly against admission of Pakistan to the UN in 1947. It later relented and voted to admit its neighbor. But on July 26,

1949, a *loyah jirgah* in Kabul formally and specifically abrogated all of its international treaties that supported the Durand Line as a border or that referred to the status of the Pashtuns.[9]

In the early stages of their campaign to liberate and/or annex Pashtunistan, the Afghans had the support of the Indian government. When as one part of this campaign the Afghans agitated for a new plebiscite that would offer independence as one of the choices, the Indians became less enthusiastic. They had, after all, adopted a policy of firm rebuff to all suggestions that the fate of Kashmir be decided on such a basis. Perhaps as a result, their support for a Pashtun plebiscite waned in the early 1950s.[10]

For the United States, relations with Pakistan and the perceived need to involve that country in one or more pacts aimed at containing the USSR took precedence over other considerations in the region. Regardless of the legitimacy of the Afghan case, the United States could not afford to antagonize the Pakistanis by supporting calls for an independent Pashtunistan.

Support offered by the USSR for Afghan claims during this period was neither enthusiastic nor effective. Having suffered some humiliation in being expelled from Iranian Azerbaidzhan in 1946, the USSR was cautious in its policies in the region. Furthermore, the Afghans had become aware of Soviet operations in the late 1940s involving the infiltration of Central Asian Tadzhik, Uzbek, and Turkomen agents into Afghanistan to contact relatives there for purposes of espionage and subversion. The targets, themselves former Basmachis and refugees from forced collectivization, did not make good subjects for such approaches, and turned in many of these agents.[11] Such operations made the Afghans doubly cautious in seeking Soviet support. (Soviet-Afghan relations, however, were good in other respects: in 1946 the border with the USSR was formally fixed as the center of the main channel of the Amu Darya and in 1947 there was an agreement to establish a telegraph link between Kabul and Tashkent.[12])

Thus the Afghans found themselves with little international support in pressing their Pashtunistan claims. This did not deter them from making inflammatory propaganda broadcasts in an effort to rouse the Pashtun tribes on the Pakistani side of the border into rebellion, nor did it deter them from infiltrating their own agents into the NWFP. By 1950 these activities had evolved into the dispatch of army irregulars across the border to attack Pakistani outposts, and after one such attack in 1950, the Pakistanis retaliated by unofficially closing their border to Afghan transport: Afghan trucks suddenly became subject to safety inspections and were found to be substandard.[13] Inasmuch as the Afghans were dependent on imports via Pakistan for virtually all products but food, their economy was in danger of coming to a complete halt. The cut off of gasoline and kerosene supplies was a particularly serious development.

At this point the USSR finally appeared to recognize the opportunity Afghanistan's short-sighted Pashtunistan policy was affording them. On July 17, 1950, a Soviet-Afghan agreement was signed. It provided for an exchange of Afghan agricultural products in return for Soviet petroleum products, cotton cloth, sugar, and other commodities.[14] In addition, the agreement provided for duty-free transit of Afghan goods over Soviet territory.[15]

Although this agreement established the first Soviet-Afghan trade link since the 1930s, it was still essentially only a barter arrangement and did not involve an active Soviet effort at economic penetration. It did cause Afghan trading patterns to change, however, and although the Pakistanis relented within three months of starting their blockade, Afghan international commerce never again reverted entirely to the old channels.

Furthermore, the agreement led the USSR to experiment with applying political leverage on Afghanistan. In the early 1950s, according to one authority, the USSR "offered" to take over from a Swedish company oil exploration in northern Afghanistan.[16] According to another authority, the oil exploration was a UN project to which the USSR raised objections in 1952 because it feared for the security of its industrial complexes in Central Asia. The Afghans appealed quietly to the United States for political support in rebuffing this objection, but they met with refusal.[17]

On this same subject the Soviets were later to confirm that in August 1952 they tendered to the Afghans a formal objection to the presence of "foreign specialists from NATO countries" in northern Afghanistan "in view of the growing striving of western intelligence to gain access and have a free hand" in that area. In reply, the Afghan government stated that NATO specialists would henceforth be barred from the northern regions.[18]

During this period the Afghans also made overtures to the United States for aid in modernizing their armed forces. Before responding, the United States checked quietly with the Pakistanis, assuring them that if U.S. military aid elsewhere in the region were felt to be threatening, Pakistan could receive additional American materiel. Having obtained Pakistan's agreement on this, the United States suggested to Kabul that if Afghanistan joined a U.S.-sponsored regional security pact, military aid might be forthcoming. As a condition to their agreement to this pact, the Afghans asked for a specific commitment by the United States to defend Afghanistan's northern border against a Soviet military thrust or even against large-scale Soviet subversion. In part because of the impossibility of honoring any such commitment, the United States turned down this proposal, and negotiations lapsed.[19] It is an open question in any case whether Afghan traditional neutrality would have permitted them to join any security pact. Later, under Daoud, Afghanistan would make public its own version of these negotiations—calling the U.S. refusal arbitrary and omitting all reference to possible Soviet aggression—to justify its acceptance of Soviet military aid.[20]

Thus it was that Afghanistan was subjected to a series of reinforcing impulses that worked to break down its traditional closed-door policy against its northern neighbor: (1) the isolation and alienation from the West that the Pashtunistan issue had brought about, (2) the initial disappointments and difficulty in financing the Helmand Valley project, and (3) the U.S. rejection of requests first for political support and then for military aid. Despite its traditional suspicions of Russian motives, pragmatic considerations were forcing Afghanistan into a closer accommodation with the USSR.

CHAPTER
4

The Soviet Drive for Economic Penetration
1953–1963

Like 1929, 1953 was an important turning point for Afghanistan both in terms of local developments and because of events far from its borders.

The end of the Korean War saw the United States briefly inclined to look more to its domestic situation than to foreign involvements. By contrast, the death of Stalin in the USSR ushered in an era of more flexible and sophisticated Soviet foreign policy. This development was to affect Afghanistan fundamentally.

For most Afghans, the most important national event of the year was the decision by the ranking members of the ruling family, the Mohammedzais, to entrust management of the Afghan state to the hands of Sardar ("Prince") Mohammed Daoud, a first cousin of King Zahir and the commander of the Afghan Army Central Forces garrison. Daoud took office as prime minister on September 20, 1953, and remained in that position for nearly ten years.

Daoud's rise to power marked the end of a tentative three-year experiment (from 1949 to 1952) in political reform by Prime Minister Shah Mahmud. Since 1931 Afghanistan had gone through the motions of periodic parliamentary elections, but the results were traditionally predetermined by the ruling elite in Kabul. Shah Mahmud made no essential change in that process, but in 1949 he did see to it that among those candidates chosen for the Seventh National Assembly there was a significant contingent with a liberal upbringing: of 120 members of parliament, between 40 and 50 were dedicated to reform, and these embarked on a program to disrupt traditional patterns of corruption among cabinet ministers.[1]

As the 1952 elections approached, however, the more extreme oppositionists overstepped the bounds of good taste and political prudence by attacking not only the government but also the royal family and even the Muslim religion. Accordingly, the government banned the three opposition newspapers that had been allowed to publish under a law passed by the reform-minded members of parliament, and they arrested the twenty-five most vocal reform leaders. About half of these subsequently agreed to cease antigovernment activities and were released from jail. Some even reached high positions in the government under Daoud.[2] Others did not survive their prison ordeal, while still others were finally released by King Zahir as part of a general amnesty in 1963.[3]

The decision to seek closer relations with the USSR was probably a collegiate one, taken in the highest councils of the Mohammedzais. To implement it and at the same time keep the reins of power in family hands, they had to choose a family member who could work both directly and via his associates with the Soviets. Ideally, such an individual should not be tainted by previous association with Afghan governments that had been cool toward the USSR. At the same time he must have the cleverness and forcefulness of character to override Afghan conservative, traditionalist opposition to the new approach. Finally, despite an ability to deal with the Soviets, he must be immune to their blandishments and remain a true Afghan nationalist. There was only one such individual, the forty-three-year-old Mohammed Daoud, son of the assassinated Afghan envoy to Germany and nephew of assassinated King Nader Shah.

Daoud was an authoritarian figure who believed in achieving social and economic progress by executive decree rather than democratic consensus. He had the reputation of crushing opposition with swift, ruthless efficiency, and although some trappings of democracy remained in Kabul (parliament was not formally abolished, for example), Daoud and a few close colleagues ran the country without much recourse to debate or compromise. He appears to have concluded that simultaneous political and economic development of Afghanistan was impossible, and to have made a clear choice in favor of economic growth.[4]

Within four months of his accession to power, in the first agreement of its kind between the two countries since the early 1920s, the USSR advanced Afghanistan a $3.5 million credit for the construction of two grain silos, a flour mill, and a bakery. The terms were generous: Afghan repayment was to be made in its natural exports, wool and cotton, and was to start only three years later, on January 1, 1957; it was to consist of five equal payments bearing an interest rate of 3 percent.[5]

As an initial foray into the field of economic assistance, the Soviet project had much to recommend it: high visibility (the twenty-thousand-ton capacity grain silos in Kabul and Pul-e-Khumri are still by far the tallest structures in each town), quick results (all buildings were completed in two years), and a purpose that was both egalitarian and humanitarian (to even out the supply and hence the price of wheat over the year). On the other hand, the bakery produced a Western-style bread that was not to Afghan taste, and it absorbed a significant percentage of the meager Afghan wheat supplies.[6]

This first Soviet effort was followed in July 1954 with a technical aid and credit agreement of $1.2 million for construction of a gasoline pipeline across the Amu Darya River from the USSR and for erection of four gasoline bulk storage tanks, with a one-million-gallon total capacity, at widely dispersed points in Afghanistan.[7]

Both of these projects had clear implications for Afghanistan's ability to weather another Pashtunistan crisis like that of 1950: if Pakistan again closed the border, the silos could store strategic food reserves for the population, while the pipeline and fuel tanks could serve a similar purpose for the economy.

In August 1954, the USSR scored a propaganda coup by agreeing to finance the paving of Kabul's streets, a project that the United States Import-Export Bank had rejected a year earlier.[8] To this end the USSR advanced a $2 million credit to be used for asphalting and road-building equipment. That same month the Czechs provided a $5 million, eight-year, 3 percent loan with which to build three cement plants—a project the Afghans had been trying unsuccessfully to negotiate with the Germans and Americans for two decades.[9]

While the USSR and its Czech ally were active with these projects in Afghanistan, the United States was engaged in improving Pakistan's defense potential. A U.S. military survey team arrived in Pakistan in March 1954 to assess the country's future military needs, and before the end of the 1954 fiscal year, the United States had committed $21 million in U.S. arms aid to it.[10] In September 1954, Pakistan joined the South East Asia Treaty Organization (SEATO) and the following year it joined the Baghdad Pact (later CENTO), thus becoming a key link in the chain of mutual security pacts the United States was forging to contain Soviet expansion.

In view of their hostile relations with Pakistan, the Afghans looked with a good deal of misgiving on the U.S. support for its rival's military forces. By this time, Afghanistan's closer relations with the USSR would have ruled out any Afghan participation in a regional pact aimed at containing her northern neighbor, even if there had been no tradition of nonalignment to uphold. At the same time, the United States could scarcely afford to arm an irredentist Afghanistan that had pretensions to Pakistani territory without some very good guarantees the U.S. arms were not going to be used against its security pact colleague. One source says that the Afghans made several requests for U.S. arms aid in the period 1953–55, but if so, U.S. refusal was a foregone conclusion.[11]

Whatever the chances of U.S. arms aid to Afghanistan might have been, they were sharply reduced by a renewed eruption of violence over Pashtunistan. In the spring of 1955, Afghan mobs were permitted if not encouraged by the authorities to tear down the flag from the Pakistani Embassy in Kabul and from its consulates in Jalalabad and Kandahar and to loot those establishments. Pakistan promptly withdrew its ambassador, suspended Afghanistan's transit privileges,[12] and unleashed its own mob violence against Afghan businesses and officials in Pakistan.[13] The border remained closed for five months until the United States finally prevailed on the Pakistanis to allow transit of U.S. aid materials and equipment to the Helmand Valley.[14] The United States turned down as impractical, however, an Afghan request to build over a thousand miles of highway through Iran to give Afghanistan an alternative route to the sea.[15]

At any rate, American support to Pakistan had caused Afghan public opinion against the United States to run so high that there were threats of turning the Helmand Valley project over to Soviet engineers.[16] By contrast, the USSR enjoyed a favorable reputation: on June 28, 1955, the Afghans negotiated a new agreement on duty-free transit of Afghan goods across Soviet territory, based on Article 6 of the 1921 treaty between the two countries.[17] On August 27, 1955, the USSR implicitly guaranteed sale of Afghanistan's fruit crop (imperiled because of the Pakistani transit stoppage) by agreeing to a new barter agreement.[18]

Western analysts of the Afghan scene are divided on the interrelationship between the Pashtunistan issue and the Afghan accommodation with the USSR. Some tend to separate the two, ascribing Daoud's move toward the USSR to his desire to achieve a more truly nonaligned position by redressing a purported Westward leaning to Afghan economic and political policy under Shah Mahmud. They lay the Pashtunistan propaganda to Daoud's belief that Shah Mahmud had not pushed the issue vigorously enough.[19] Others suggest that Daoud may have fostered the Pashtunistan issue deliberately for the specific purpose of justifying his turning to the USSR for economic and, especially, military aid.[20] Certainly the worsening relations with the United States must have helped overcome the trepidations of conservative Afghans regarding acceptance of assistance from the USSR.

By November Pakistan had lifted its embargo, but the way had been prepared for a quantum jump in Soviet-Afghan relations. In December 1955, at the end of a tour of southeast Asia, Nikita Khrushchev and Nikolay Bulganin, leaders of the Soviet Party and the Soviet State, respectively, stopped off in Kabul. During their visit, they announced the granting of a $100 million, long-term development loan to Afghanistan. Simultaneously, the 1931 treaty of friendship and nonaggression was extended for ten years.[21]

The formal agreement was signed in January 1956. It provided for Afghan repayment to be made at the rate of 2 percent per year over twenty-two equal annual payments, with payments to start eight years after the loan was granted. Payment was to be made in Afghan goods, with prices to be determined by world market prices at the time of delivery. The nature and quantity of goods to be exchanged would be determined by mutual consent on an annual basis.[22]

It has been noted that the Soviet offer of aid to Afghanistan paralleled similar offers by the USSR to other countries during this same general time frame: 400 million rubles to Argentina in 1958, $100 million to Cuba in 1960, and one $100-million loan to Indonesia and another to Ethiopia.[23] From the perspective of the 1980s, the USSR's political profit from these investments appears to have been nil in Indonesia, marginal in Argentina, and seemingly an outright success in

Cuba and Ethiopia. The return on the Afghan investment is still open to question.

From the standpoint of the Afghans, acceptance of the Soviet loan violated their isolationist traditions far more significantly than had similar acceptance of American aid for the Helmand Valley project. In the 1930s Afghanistan had solicited foreign assistance on a modest scale from developed countries, but only from those whose distance from Afghanistan's borders had provided some insurance against a political/ military follow-up to the economic investment. Afghan requests for German, Italian, and Japanese technological help before World War II, for example, were based less on any pro-Axis political bias than on Afghan unwillingness to give their two most powerful neighbors, the British and the Russians, any kind of economic foothold in their country. The postwar approach to the United States was based in good part on the same considerations.

As the dimensions and direction of the Soviet involvement emerged over the next months, the extent of Afghanistan's departure from established policies became ever clearer. In the 1890s Abdur Rahman had warned specifically of the dangers that a railroad would pose for his country's independence. In March 1956, the projects selected by a joint Afghan-Soviet survey team, while not involving railroads, were associated to a large extent with creating and modernizing other transportation facilities. There were two airport projects, one major highway (linking Kabul with the Soviet border), one river port facility improvement project (where the proposed highway would cross into the USSR), construction of one modern bridge, and improvement and construction of three auto repair workshops. Other projects under consideration included a materials testing laboratory in Kabul, two hydroelectric stations, three irrigation dams, and a fertilizer factory.[24] Some of these were deemed impractical and shelved.[25] That same March an air agreement was signed that provided for regular flights between Tashkent and Kabul.[26]

A curious example of Soviet defensive concerns was included in Article IV of this agreement: "Each side has the right to refuse or amend flight permission to the other if it does not have proof that the majority ownership or actual control of that enterprise is being realized by citizens or organs of that country. . . ." In other words, the burden of proof would be on Ariana Afghan Airlines to prove that it was not owned and/or controlled by a foreign concern. In fact, 49 percent of Ariana stock at that time was owned by Peter Baldwin, an American entrepreneur who actually started that airline in April 1955.[27] Later, in 1957, Pan American Airways bought out Baldwin for $400 thousand, and for more than two decades thereafter was active in helping Ariana with its operations and maintenance problems.[28]

Also in March 1956, the Afghans signed an agreement calling for Soviet specialists to be stationed in Afghanistan for the purpose of setting up, maintaining, and repairing various equipment in connection with the aid projects, and training their Afghan colleagues in its use. These specialists were also supposed to oversee Afghan construction activities according to approved project plans.[29]

The greatest break with tradition, however, came with the August 1956 agreement on reequipping Afghanistan's armed forces with Soviet materiel. Of necessity, given the complexity of modern armaments, this agreement involved the training of Afghan officers in Soviet military schools and the stationing of Soviet experts at Afghan military bases. The opportunity this gave the USSR for assessing and recruiting individual officers to serve Soviet political aims is self evident, and it was not ignored.

Though many observers of the Afghan scene feared even then that Daoud was leading his country into Soviet vassalage, others perceived in his actions a high-risk gamble to improve his country's lot by playing off the Great Powers against each other. In fact, one analyst termed Afghanistan an "economic Korea," where the competition between East and West benefited a local population without endangering its independence.[30] And indeed, Afghanistan did profit in the short run as a result of competing aid programs: hardly had the agreements with the USSR been concluded in early 1956 than the United States was also offering official aid. (Before that time the Afghans had secured individual commercial loans in the West, but these were not connected with overall U.S. policy; official aid had been on a very small scale.) U.S. projects included road building, airport construction, further progress on the Helmand Valley project, and long-term educational activities (rural schools, textbooks, and the like). In addition, the United States donated one hundred thirty thousand tons of wheat to Afghanistan in the period 1956–59, under the terms of PL-480-II, whereas in 1952–54, before the sharp increase in Soviet aid, it had *sold* them just twenty thousand tons.[31]

The U.S. position in expanding the Afghan share of foreign aid was explicit. It was aimed at securing "maximum internal political stability, promoting friendly economic relations with her (Afghanistan's) Free World neighbors, and minimizing any possibility that Afghanistan might either be a victim of, or a pathway for, Soviet domination in South Asia."[32]

In the period 1950–59, U.S. assistance totaled $148.3 million, while Soviet assistance came to $246.2 million. While most of the U.S. assistance was in the form of outright grants, the USSR concentrated more on long-term loans.[33] Although the United States did not try to match the volume of the Soviet assistance, the impact of the U.S. projects was considerable, and most Western analysts seem to feel that the Afghans benefited as much from the U.S. aid as from the Soviet.[34]

On the other hand, between 1950 and 1960 Afghan dependence on the USSR had risen from nothing to 100 percent for arms, from perhaps 10 percent to 90 percent for petroleum products, and from 17 percent (1951) to nearly 50 percent for total foreign trade.[35]

Despite the development of these strategic vulnerabilities, Afghanistan continued to maintain its nonaligned status, and Daoud made a point of emphasizing continued Afghan freedom, independence, and neutrality as leading items on his list of national priorities. Economic progress was invariably listed as a secondary aim in his speeches.[36]

During the 1950s there was little direct evidence that Soviet ambitions in Afghanistan went beyond ensuring that the country continue to perform its traditional buffer-state role. The strategic significance of the Soviet highway project that ran from the Soviet border at Kushka to Herat and Kandahar, linking up there with the U.S. highway to Kabul, however, was not lost on Western observers. One, who saw Soviet aims in Afghanistan as similar to those of the United States, noted that it might allow an aggressor to transport supplies and men directly to the Pakistan border—"provided he has Afghan consent."[37]

Only careful examination of agreements made during those years and of their subsequent implementation gives evidence of long-range Soviet intentions. Article 21 of the border agreement of January 18, 1958, for example, stipulated that on forty-eight-hour notice either side could examine those parts of international bridges linking the two countries that were located on the other side's territory.[38] Should the Afghans have wanted to mine these links as a defensive measure, Soviet inspectors would soon have discovered that fact. The May 30,

1959, agreement on building the Kushka-Kandahar road was followed in July by a specific agreement that dealt only with building three new bridges—across the Besuda, Kameh, and Asmar Rivers. Construction of the bridges was to involve Afghan labor working under the immediate supervision of Soviet engineers.[39] Afghan engineers were to comment subsequently on the overstrength capability of such bridges in relation to the heaviest Afghan civilian truck traffic, American military attachés on bridges capable of supporting the heaviest of Soviet battle tanks.[40]

The U.S. commitment to Afghanistan in the last years of the decade was deliberately ambiguous. In early 1957 the visit to Kabul by Special Presidential Assistant James P. Richards resulted in a communiqué that confirmed U.S. support for Afghanistan's continued independence, but did not state whether or not the country was protected by the Eisenhower Doctrine (i.e., whether it would enjoy U.S. armed support in the event of a Soviet invasion).[41]

Insofar as the USSR might have hoped for a political return on its economic investment, however, the signs were not encouraging. A visit to Kabul by President Eisenhower in December 1959 was a widely hailed success. In an obvious move to obtain equal coverage, Khrushchev visited Kabul in early 1960 and reportedly offered to finance the entire Afghan second Five Year Plan if the Afghans would agree to the presence of Soviet advisors in all their ministries. Daoud is said to have rejected this alleged offer outright.[42] Not only was the United States enjoying a good reputation, but it even appeared for a short time that Afghan-Pakistani relations might be mending. A 1960 compact between the countries was designed to settle problems and bring tranquility to the border.[43] This apparent move toward reconciliation, however, proved to be illusory.

In early 1959 the Afghan foreign minister had gone to Pakistan for talks, but the mission was not a success, and differences between the two countries again began to become more noticeable.[44] Afghan propaganda in Pakistani territory intensified, and after some delay it was countered with Pakistani propaganda beamed at Afghan listeners. As relations worsened, these exchanges evolved into official harassment (for example, Pakistani nationals were no longer issued residence permits by Afghan authorities after May 1960), and finally, in September 1960, there were armed incursions into Pakistan by Afghan irregulars disguised as tribesmen.[45] In May 1961 a similar force launched an abortive raid in support of the Nawab of Dir, on the Pakistani side of the Durand Line.[46]

In August 1961, citing as a reason Afghan harassment of its consulates in Jalalabad and Kandahar, Pakistan shut down these installations. At the same time they demanded that the Afghans close their corresponding consulates in Parichinar, Peshawar, and Quetta, on the grounds that these were fomenting sedition in Pakistan. The Afghans gave the Pakistanis a one-week ultimatum to reconsider this move, after which, on September 6, 1961, they broke diplomatic relations. The border was again shut down, and as in the past, trade was rerouted via the USSR. Just ten days after the border closed, Daoud's brother and confidant, Sardar Mohammed Naim, flew to Moscow and returned with the promise of a Soviet airlift to remove Afghanistan's perishable fruit harvest, which had been stranded by the transportation blockage.[47] Within a month, the USSR again reportedly offered Afghanistan loans and credits totaling $450 million for their second Five Year Plan. This was virtually the entire amount needed.[48] If this offer was indeed made, the Afghans understood its implications for the future of their independence and turned it down.

Even without their acceptance, however, the break in relations with Pakistan was clearly a desirable development from Moscow's standpoint. Afghan gratitude for the Soviet rescue of their fruit harvest was one benefit. Renewed Afghan isolation and alienation from the West was another, as U.S. aid projects faltered from the shutdown in the flow of supplies. The trend of the late 1950s toward an accommodation with Pakistan was reversed.

The extent to which the USSR might have had a hand in promoting the diplomatic break can only be conjectured. Some aspects of the conflict as it developed in the border areas along the Durand Line had a decidedly alien flavor, however.

As propaganda degenerated into actual fighting, Afghan authorities gave a bounty to Pakistani Pashtuns for each empty rifle shell and grenade pin claimed to have been used in battle against Pakistani regular forces; in addition to this, they also provided replacement munitions.[49] For Afghan authorities to have made such an offer to the hill tribesmen, who loved hunting and were customarily at war only with each other, was to display either unusual naïveté or unlimited resources or both. Furthermore, for those who wished to amass a reserve against future needs, replacement of a standard grenade pin with an old piece of wire or used cotter pin ensured a steadily mounting stock of valuable—if not entirely safe—munitions.

Those in power in Kabul were themselves Pashtuns, and could have been under no illusions as to the ultimate disposition of most of the supplies that the Afghan Army was dispensing to Pakistani Pashtuns with such a lavish hand. It is therefore not unreasonable to assume that the guarantee of the material resources to carry out this program, if not the very concept of the program itself, were of Soviet origin. In fact, the visit of Soviet Marshal Vassiliy Danilovich Sokolovskiy to Kabul in October 1961, the specific purposes of which were never made public, may have had some connection with the program.[50]

From 1961 to 1963, diplomatic relations between Afghanistan and Pakistan remained ruptured. The economic effects of the border closure were slow in coming, but eventually they began to affect the population at large. The loss of customs duty at the Pakistani border removed the single largest source of government revenues, and the country's hard currency reserves sank sharply. Eventually matters reached such a critical stage that the king asked Daoud to resign, and in March 1963, the latter obeyed.[51] Within two months diplomatic relations were reestablished with Pakistan, and the border was again opened.

For the USSR, Daoud's departure was a definite setback. The goals of Soviet economic and military aid programs had been the establishment of an Afghan client-state relationship, with Kabul dependent on Moscow for marketing its exports, supplying its military forces, backing its international political claims (Pashtunistan), and modernizing its economy. On all of these issues Daoud's policies had seemed to be largely in line with Soviet aspirations, even if they had been neither avowedly nor secretly pro-Soviet.

As long as Daoud remained in power and his policies remained in force, the USSR could assume that Soviet influence would grow and Afghan dependence would increase, intensifying whenever the Pashtunistan issue became heated. In the end, it could be anticipated that the USSR would come to have a dominating political influence in the country, in both domestic and foreign relations.

For Daoud, opening the door to Soviet aid programs had been a calculated risk. It had brought increased U.S. aid to offset the Soviet effort, thus providing a double economic benefit while lessening the dangers of a total dependence on the USSR. At the same time, it had opened the door for Soviet subversion via the Afghan military forces that were trained, equipped, and advised by Soviet mentors. Daoud unquestionably recognized this danger, but apparently believed he could handle it through his own command of the army's loyalty, the patriotism of the Afghan citizenry, and the innate suspicion with which Afghans viewed Russians.

If the USSR had had any illusions that Daoud's personal ambitions outweighed his patriotism, they must have been dissipated when Daoud quietly and obediently stepped down at the request of King Zahir. This was no surprise move by the king, designed to catch Daoud off guard. On the contrary, it was deliberately floated as a rumor from the royal palace some weeks before in order to gauge the people's reaction in advance. When the response showed that a change would indeed be popular, the king made his move.

Daoud might have defied his sovereign and stayed on. He appeared to have the loyalty of the army (the ultimate source of political power in the country) and he had the time to organize a coup. If he had done so, it is difficult to imagine who could have stood in his way. Domestically he controlled the guns, and abroad he was assured of support by the USSR, the only foreign neighbor in a credible position to intervene. He chose instead to step down without resistance, but with a farewell address that did much to revive his flagging popularity among the civilian population.[52]

According to one analyst, there were three groups of people who were genuinely sorry to see Daoud step down: (1) those who ardently supported the Pashtunistan issue, (2) some members of the royal family who stood to lose lucrative positions in the government, and (3) "those few army officers and intellectuals committed to the Soviet line."[53]

From the Soviet standpoint there were few options available through which they might have salvaged their position. The logical personality around whom a coup might have been staged had removed himself from the political scene and there was no one else of any stature over whom the USSR had adequate influence. Direct military intervention was not an attractive alternative in early 1963, only a few months after the United States had faced down the USSR in Cuba, though analysts at the time did not completely rule out that possibility.[54]

Economic aid had proven to be an effective foreign policy tool, but

by itself it had not been enough to establish a dominant Soviet influence in Afghanistan. For the next fifteen years the economic
penetration effort would continue, but manipulation of internal *political* forces was to occupy an apparently ever more important place in
Soviet strategic thinking on Afghanistan.

CHAPTER

5

The Drive for
Political Control: 1
"Democratic" Political Influence
1963–1973

When Daoud took power in 1953, he established a regime that was intolerant of opposition from any quarter. The memory of the anarchic Seventh National Assembly (1949–52) was still fresh, and Daoud's relationship even to his own ministers was less that of a senior colleague than of "a general dealing with his sergeants."[1]

As a result, an inchoate coalition of disparate elements built up against him and eventually contributed to his resignation in 1963. The very success of his programs and Afghanistan's economic advancement was another contributing factor in his fall; as the economy expanded, there was an ever greater need for delegation of decision-making to lower and lower levels. At the same time, improvements in education had led to the formation of a larger and larger body of trained young people who wanted a voice in managing their country's affairs. One-man rule was becoming both unpopular and inefficient.

In Daoud's place, the king had appointed Mohammed Yousuf, minister of mines and industries, to take over the reins of government pending the drafting of a new constitution. In appointing Yousuf, who was no relation to himself, the king let it be known that in the future the royal family could "lay down its burden of a generation and let the Afghan educated class run the country."[2] This principle became a matter of law in Article 24 of the constitution, the fifth paragraph of which stated, "Members of the Royal House shall not hold the follow-

ing offices: Prime Minister or Minister, Member of Parliament, Justice
of the Supreme Court."[3]

The 1964 constitution was the final product of eighteen months of
effort by a drafting commission and ten days of intense debate in a
loyah jirgah. What emerged was a consensus document that appeared
to have good prospects of success. Following its ratification and signa-
ture by the king (on October 1, 1964), the new constitution laid the
groundwork for a parliamentary monarchy that included many traditional democratic principles developed in the West—separation of
powers, elections by secret ballot, and presumption of innocence in
court, to name a few. As in other Muslim countries, however, there
was explicit linking of church and state, and for the time being civil
rights received only cursory attention. Nevertheless, the constitution
did provide an apparently stable base on which a democratic state
could have been built. Laws governing the establishment of political
parties were supposed to be developed in the first freely elected
parliament, and a press law, restrictive by Western standards but very
liberal in the Afghan context, was passed in July 1965. There was even
provision for feminine rights in the constitution, and the *loyah jirgah*
itself had four woman participants.[4]

Even if there had been no group hostile to the concept of constitutional monarchy and dedicated to its overthrow, democracy would
have led a perilous existence during its formative years in Afghanistan.
There was at least 90 percent illiteracy in the country; communications
systems were rudimentary; organizations that cut across family or
tribal lines were virtually nonexistent; loyalties and hostilities alike
were fierce, local, and personal; and there was no popular sense of
national unity or nationwide awareness of common problems. In fact, it
is surprising that the democratic experiment did manage to struggle on
for ten years before again succumbing to one-man rule.

As educated Afghans wrestled with the new concepts of government, four general ideological positions emerged among the informed
electorate: *traditionalists* wished to retain Afghan culture under firm,
traditional Islamic principles; *adaptors* wanted somehow to meld
Western technology and managerial practices with Afghan culture and
Islamic teachings; *democrats* looked forward to a democratic republic
and put their faith in following Western models more directly; and
Marxist-Leninists were by definition committed in theory to eventual
revolutionary overthrow of any noncommunist government.[5] With the

exception of the last, all had political roots that went directly back to the World War I era of pan-Islamism and even beyond.

To trace Marxist-Leninist roots in Afghanistan we must look back again briefly to the violence-prone Young Afghan movement of the early 1930s and the Seventh National Assembly of the late 1940s. Although the Young Afghans as a group did not adopt Marxism-Leninism as a creed, in 1947 some of the group's former members formed a successor organization called the Wikh-i-Zalmayan ("Awakened Youth"), which included a number of pro-Soviet elements. The Awakened Youth was formed in protest against abuses of power by the leading Mohammedzai family members who ran the country, and it went on to play a prominent role in the politics of the Seventh National Assembly. The key figures around whom this opposition coalesced were Mir Ghulam Mohammed Ghubar (who had been arrested in connection with Nader Shah's assassination) and Dr. Abdur Rahman Mahmudi.[6]

Mahmudi was active in launching the opposition newspaper *Watan* ("Homeland"), the organ of the embryonic Watan party which was led by himself and Ghubar. Another collaborator in the journal was Babrak Karmal, a future communist ruler of Afghanistan.[7] Mahmudi, who was born in 1909, was elected to the Seventh National Assembly and was also active in founding another newspaper, *Nida-i-Khalq* ("Voice of the Masses"), which was banned after twenty-nine issues. Both in its name and its political orientation (leftist but conceding the practical need for temporary accommodation with the monarchy) this paper was a forerunner of the more outspokenly communist outlet, *Khalq*.

In 1952 Mahmudi and sixteen of his followers were arrested. Mahmudi's health was broken as a result of severe beatings by the police and prison authorities. In 1963, following Daoud's removal from power Mahmudi was released from jail, but he died only a few months later.[8]

The year Mahmudi died was also the year Nur Mohammed Taraki began holding meetings with other leftist figures to form a new political party. Starting in September 1963, these meetings were to continue through December of the following year. They culminated in a gathering at Taraki's home in the Shah Mina district of Kabul on January 1, 1965, at which the People's Democratic Party of Afghanistan (PDPA) was officially founded. About thirty persons attended, twenty of whom were elected as either full or alternate members of the PDPA's Central

Committee. The host, Taraki, was unanimously elected secretary general. If the gestation of organized communist political activity can be dated from Taraki's preliminary meetings, the formal birth of the Afghan communist party (even though the term communist is not used in its title) can be established as New Year's Day, 1965.

The details of what went on at the preliminary meetings are obscure; the fact that they took place at all only came to light in 1979—and in the West at that.[9] As late as 1960, an American researcher was to base his conclusion that "Soviet political aims in Afghanistan do not seem to differ much from those of the United States" in part on the fact that there is "no open or clandestine communist propaganda in Afghanistan."[10]

The specific ideological orientation of the PDPA, however, was clear from the very beginning: "Its programme," a leftist journal was to report later, "was an orthodox Communist one for the period, reflecting analyses associated with Khrushchev or Brezhnev."[11] A year later, its official organ, *Khalq*, was to declare the PDPA's goal as the "further development of the great October Revolution in Afghanistan."[12] Given the PDPA's unswerving subsequent support to any and all Soviet initiatives, the source of its inspiration would not have been difficult to deduce even without this declaration.

Following its formation as an organization, the PDPA was quick to apply its revolutionary doctrine in practice. By the end of the following summer, elections to the Lower House of Parliament ("Wolesi Jirgah") had resulted in victories for a few PDPA officials, including Central Committee members Babrak Karmal, Anahita Ratebzad (one of four women elected to the Lower House), and Nur Ahmad Nur. Nur Mohammed Taraki and Hafizullah Amin ran but did not win their contests. Due to the numerical insignificance of leftist representation in Parliament, PDPA policy was to sabotage that body's work rather than to operate within it.

Pending convocation of Parliament, the king had continued to put his faith in Mohammed Yousuf, the interim prime minister who had been acting since Daoud's departure in 1963. After the elections, the king asked Yousuf to form a new government, which he did. When the new government was presented to Parliament for confirmation, however, the proposed ministers were subjected to several days of unbridled abuse by the newly elected members of Parliament. Babrak and Anahita led the anti-Yousuf protest, which reached such a pitch of vituperation that Yousuf finally asked that either formal charges be leveled against him and his ministers in a court of law, or an end be called to the denunciations that had included charges of bribery, corruption, nepotism, and the like. He requested that his new cabinet be subjected to a vote of confidence in three days' time.[13]

If the vote had been taken immediately, Dr. Yousuf might well have won it without difficulty. As it was, three days was adequate for Babrak to mobilize his sympathizers among the Kabul student body. A student sit-in staged by him and his supporters forced Parliament to cancel a scheduled meeting on October 24, the day the new cabinet was to be approved. The following day, Parliament met in closed session, and overwhelmingly voted in favor of the Yousuf government. The fact that the session was closed however, touched off riots in which three students were killed. Yousuf immediately resigned, and on October 29 Parliament elected Mohammed Hashim Maiwandwal as prime minister in his place. (Only seven votes were cast against the choice of Maiwandwal; true to the PDPA policy of disruption, the same seven votes were to be the only ones registered against Prime Minister Etemadi in a vote of confidence in 1967.[14])

The student riots were a development that set back the cause of democracy in Afghanistan perhaps more than any other single event in the 1960s. The extent to which the USSR had a direct hand in the riots is open to question. Certainly the PDPA took its overall ideological guidance from Moscow, and it is reasonable to assume that there was local PDPA contact with the Soviet Embassy in Kabul for immediate questions of tactics and strategy. This does not necessarily imply a fully coordinated Soviet control over the PDPA, however, and there is some evidence that the USSR was embarrassed vis-à-vis the Third World by the violent turn the demonstrations took. In 1966 one Soviet author, writing in English (i.e., for non-Soviet audiences), euphemistically referred to the riots only as ". . . actions of an oppositionist nature . . . (which) caused certain difficulties in forming the new cabinet. . . ."[15] On the other hand, the same author, writing this time in Russian for Soviet audiences, dealt with the riots less elliptically and with some implicit approval, noting that they followed Leninist teachings on the revolutionary role of the intelligentsia.[16]

Although the new prime minister managed to become popular among the students by appearing at the memorial service for those who had been killed, PDPA agitation in the student body resulted in new violence before the end of the year. Starting on December 9, leftist leaders instigated anti-German demonstrations, aimed against the West German educational assistance program and alleged misconduct by West German visiting educators in the science faculty.[17] These demonstrations met with generally tepid support by the student body at large, even though the sentencing of a leftist teacher, Mohammed Osman, also from the science faculty, to two years in prison on December 12 provided a new focus for unrest.

The Germans have generally been popular among Afghans, and the anti-German demands made by the student agitators were considered unrealistic by most students and by the population at large.[18] The role of the West Germans as whipping boys for Soviet propagandists of that day, however, may explain this ill-advised choice of target by the agitators.

Following an initial period of uncertainty, the Afghan government's response to the unrest was a forthright program of arrests and expulsions from the university of persons thought to have been responsible for fomenting disturbances. This policy had the desired sobering effect on the students in the short term, but it was at the expense of slowing and even reversing the process of democratization in the country.

In the spring of 1966, reaction against the government took a new form as six opposition newspapers came into being in response to relaxation of government censorship regulations. Only one out of the six was clearly identifiable as a communist journal. This was *Khalq* ("Masses"), published by the PDPA's secretary general, Nur Mohammed Taraki, and edited by Bareq Shafiee, a durable figure in PDPA politics.

If there had been any previous doubts as to the politico-ideological orientation of the PDPA, they should have been laid to rest by *Khalq*. Even the phraseology of its writings was alien to Afghan Persian, resembling that found in political organs in Soviet Tadzhikistan.[19] As for content, the paper followed the Soviet line both in general ideological terms ("the main issue of contemporary times and the center of class struggle on a world-wide basis is the struggle between international socialism and international imperialism, which began with the Great October Revolution") and even on such specific Soviet dogmas as the demand for socialist realism in art.[20]

The government moved quickly to suppress what it identified as a subversive journal; after six issues *Khalq* was shut down. The reasons cited were the paper's anti-Islam, antimonarchy, and anticonstitution lines, but it is probable that the government's real concern was its identification of *Khalq* as little less than a controlled Soviet outlet operating on Afghan territory. As in the case of leftist-sponsored riots the previous October, the strong countermeasures taken by the government injured more than just the truly alien target. Of the six opposition journals that appeared in the first half of 1966, only one remained at the end of the year. One had closed for financial reasons, one (founded to fight *Khalq*) ceased publication because its reason for existence had been removed, and three were shut down by government decree.[21]

After *Khalq*'s demise there was no offically sanctioned communist journal until Sulaiman Laeq began publishing *Parcham* ("Banner") in March 1968. Laeq's coeditor on *Parcham* was Mir Akbar Khyber (whose assassination ten years later was to trigger the 1978 communist coup), but its unacknowledged chief was Babrak Karmal.

In June 1967, the PDPA split into two hostile factions: the Khalqis under Nur Mohammed Taraki and the Parchamis under Babrak. There was no real ideological reason for the break: both Taraki and Babrak remained firmly loyal to Soviet-style Marxism-Leninism, and differed only slightly as to tactics.

The Khalqis put emphasis on class warfare, while the Parchamis called for a united democratic front that was supposed to work within the framework of the existing order. Both of these lines, of course, reflect tactics that communist parties in most countries have pursued at various times without ever losing sight of the ultimate strategic goal of permanently displacing the indigenous noncommunist government. In the case of Parcham and Khalq, even these differences were minor: in 1966 *Khalq* (Taraki's paper) recognized the need for the monarchy "at this stage of Afghanistan's development," scarcely a class war position.[22] For his part, Babrak gave away nothing in his efforts to gain noncommunist political allies in a United Front. It must also be recalled that Babrak had been the "class warrior" who had called the students out to disrupt Parliament, while Taraki, whatever his professed revolutionary convictions, was essentially a poet and an intellectual, not an activist.

Similarly, a purported difference in commitment to Pashtunistan (backed more consistently by the Khalqis) was more apparent than real. Inasmuch as the Khalqis were predominantly Pashtun, while the

Parchamis were more representative of all Afghan nationalities, such a difference would have been natural in any case. In fact, however, when Parchamis found it politically expedient to support Pashtunistan, they did so with just as great vigor as the Khalqis.

Babrak and Taraki each commanded the loyalty of about half of the PDPA movement, and each was to maintain an unbroken hostility toward the other for ten years—until 1977 when a seeming reconciliation, very probably imposed from outside, took place. During all this time each maintained firm loyalty to Moscow, while accusing the other of various deviations. The fundamental reason for their hostility was the personal antagonism and rivalry for control of the party by the two leaders. It was only after this had developed that somewhat artificial ideological and tactical differences were brought out as ostensible explanations for the split.

In 1968 a new wave of labor strikes and student unrest swept over the country. Again, the degree to which the USSR was directly involved cannot be determined, but neither Khalq nor Parcham was an idle bystander to the violence that erupted. In part as a reaction to these disturbances, a purported massive shift to the right occurred in the 1969 parliamentary elections.[23] For the period of the election, *Parcham* and several other opposition newspapers were banned, and there were subsequent allegations that the government interfered blatantly to secure the defeat of leftist candidates.[24] Insofar as the government may have indulged in such activities, it does not seem to have pressed its campaign with great vigor. Although Nur Ahmad Nur, who dates his PDPA membership from 1963,[25] was defeated, and Anahita Ratebzad did not run, Hafizullah Amin (defeated in 1965) did win and Babrak himself was reelected. Overall, the left did lose ground, but the cause was probably less a matter of government interference than the weakening effect of the Parcham/Khalq split on the one hand, and popular resentment against leftist disturbances on the other.

The left's popularity was further eroded when, in April 1970, *Parcham* printed an ode to Lenin on the occasion of his birthday praising him in terms normally reserved for the Prophet Mohammed. This resulted in anticommunist demonstrations by mullahs and their followers, which were met by student counterdemonstrations. The poet responsible for the ode was Bareq Shafiee, who had been editor of *Khalq* under Taraki in 1966, was working for Babrak on *Parcham* at the time of this poem, was to be minister of transport and tourism under Taraki in 1979, and as of June 1980, was again a ranking figure in the PDPA under Babrak. Such changes in allegiance are unusual and are considered improper by most Afghans; a possible reflection of this attitude is the fact that Bareq, despite his earlier prominence in the movement, has been accorded only *alternate* membership in the 1980 Babrak Central Committee and Revolutionary Council.

As the decade of the 1960s came to an end, Afghanistan's importance as an overt area for playing out the East-West struggle seems to have waned, as Vietnam came ever more to dominate the international scene. Year by year the Soviet economic investment in Afghanistan was cut back, from $44.7 million in 1967–68, to $30.5 million in 1968–69, to $28.4 million in 1969–70. During the same period, U.S. grants and loans fell even faster, from $12.7 million, to $4.8 million, to $1.4 million.[26]

Politically, those forces in Afghanistan that publicly supported the USSR became less popular. Despite its publication of the near-heretical ode to Lenin, *Parcham* was allowed to continue publication, but it did not command a large readership. Leftist strength in the Wolesi Jirgah was negligible. The prospects for a communist victory in any free election were virtually nonexistent in the foreseeable future.

These trends led some analysts to conclude that the importance of Afghanistan had been reduced in Soviet eyes. While this apparent loss of interest was developing, however, Afghan civilian students and military officers continued to be trained in the Soviet Union, where they fell under long-term scrutiny of the Soviet intelligence services. At the same time, the decrease in foreign aid had led to unemployment among the restless new intelligentsia that was being turned out in ever larger numbers by the expanded educational program. Afghanistan's fragile democracy appeared progressively less capable of handling the complex problems of a rapidly developing economy.

It is doubtful that long-term Soviet political plans in Afghanistan had changed between 1963 and 1973. Reliance on "democratic" political instruments (the PDPA, *Khalq*, and *Parcham*), however, had proven as ineffectual an approach for the USSR as reliance on purely economic penetration had shown itself during the previous decade. It was time for a new approach, one that might result in effective Soviet influence on the country's policies from behind the scenes.

The end of democracy in Afghanistan came on July 17, 1973, when

Mohammed Daoud again took over the country, this time in a nearly bloodless coup that saw the king banished into exile, the constitution abrogated, and civil liberties suspended. Afghanistan had returned to one-man rule.

CHAPTER

6

The Drive for
Political Control: 2
Political Manipulation
1973–1978

When Mohammed Daoud came to power for the second time, his takeover was virtually unopposed. The only casualties were one tank commander (who drowned when his vehicle swerved off the road to avoid collision with a bus and sank in the Kabul River), and seven policemen at one station (all of whom mistook the rebels for some other hostile force). Within hours the country was securely in Daoud's hands, and there was no armed opposition to the coup. The king was in Europe at the time, and he simply stayed there, accepting exile in Italy.

Daoud's swift success can be ascribed to classic coup prerequisites: disaffection with the existing regime by key elements of the population, his own correct perception of the government's vulnerability to overthrow, secure advance planning by the conspirators, and assurances by the military that the nation's armed forces would either remain neutral or support the coup.

The popular dissatisfactions with the monarchy were vague but pervasive. Not only were such corrupt practices as bribe-taking and nepotism flourishing as much under the *Democracy-i-nau* ("New Democracy"), just as they had under earlier regimes, but the very freedom to expose and criticize such practices (without being able to stop them) led to even greater popular discontent than before.

Daoud also recognized the factors that made democracy so frail in Afghanistan—lack of communications, low literacy rate, and the like. Perhaps the single most important weakness was the absence of any pan-Afghan organizations that would have permitted appreciation of truly national problems and inculcated in the people loyalties beyond the immediate calls of family and tribe. Political parties eventually might have filled this gap, but the only such organizations in existence in 1973 were still embryonic—the quasi-legal PDPA factions (Parcham and Khalq), the Maoist Sholaye Jaweid (Eternal Flame), and Mohammed Hashim Maiwandwal's unofficial Progressive Democratic Party (PDP), for example. Government failure to get on with passing a political parties law is in part to blame for this situation, but it is doubtful that even legal sanction would have permitted a rapid enough development of various party organizations and loyalties to have forestalled the 1973 coup.[1]

The third and probably decisive factor was the coterie of supporters that had gravitated to Daoud during the years since his last term of office. Starting in 1969, he began holding seminars to discuss what had gone wrong during his previous tenure and what might be done to correct both his own former errors and those of the present regime. Young military officers, many of them trained in the USSR and already members of Parcham or Khalq, attended these meetings, as did more moderate thinkers.[2] From the cabinet Daoud put together when the coup succeeded, it appears that most of the members of his previous (1953–63) government were ignored in the planning for his new one. Excluding his younger brother Naim (who throughout Daoud's career remained a close foreign policy advisor, with or without a formal title), the only carry-over of ministerial rank from the 1953–63 era was Dr. Abdul Majid (minister of education in 1952–57 and minister of justice 1973–77).

In place of his former ministers, Daoud appointed new people, most of them unknown on the Afghan political scene, though some had already had unpublicized experience in government. (Mohammed Hassan Sharq, for example, first deputy prime minister under Daoud in 1973, had been head of the Prime Ministry Secretariat from 1953 to 1963,[3] yet his biography is not to be found in Adamec's authoritative *Who's Who of Afghanistan.*)

Although none of these men had been a PDPA Central Committee member or alternate in 1965, no fewer than eight out of fourteen were known—then or later—as PDPA members, former members, or strong sympathizers. This category included the only two officials of ministerial rank to carry over from the previous (Shafiq) government to Daoud's without demotion. Six of the eight leftists were to hold important positions in government under Babrak Karmal in 1980: two were to be ministers; three, ambassadors; and one, advisor to the Prime Ministry. Of the other two, one was killed in the 1978 coup and the other has dropped from sight.

What brought Daoud to power, however, was not ideology but military power. He had the loyalty of key military officers, and he exploited that fact in carrying out the coup. Here again, the individuals who helped him were for the most part pro-Soviet. Of those who featured in the coup, only General Abdul Mustaghni, Major Abdul Qadir Nuristani, and Colonel Ghulam Sarwar had no leftist affiliations. Three of the pro-Soviet military officers (Pacha Gul Wafadar, Faiz Mohammed, and Abdul Hamid Mohtat) quit the army after the coup and joined Daoud's first cabinet as ministers, while four others (Abdul Qader, Aslam Watanjar, Sayed Mohammed Gulabzoy, and Shah Jan Mazdooryar) remained on as career soldiers. The latter were to play key roles in the 1978 coup that toppled Daoud himself. All seven of them, civilian and military alike, were ranking members of the communist regime in 1980. In 1973, however, they had been the key to Daoud's success.

In addition to the formal organs of state administration, Daoud's government contained a somewhat mysterious Central Committee whose functions and complete membership were never spelled out, but which seemed to act in a policy advisory role for Daoud. Of six members listed in one compilation, all but Daoud himself had pasts and/or futures of close affiliation with Marxism-Leninism.[4]

Daoud had one other very important tactical advantage. Shafiq's minister of interior, Nehmatullah Pazhwak, was a secret Parcham adherent.[5] In the two years he had served as minister of interior, Pazhwak had hired a number of young Parcham activists as policemen and as other interior ministry officials in Kabul. There were, in Kabul, about 160 of these young enthusiasts on whom Daoud could count for support in the first days of his new government.

In addition to helping Daoud after he took over, Pazhwak had also been in a position both to affect government policy under Shafiq—and to betray it. This may serve to explain why General Abdul Wali, chief of Central Forces under the king, took no action to thwart the Daoud conspirators, a list of whose identities and a description of whose intentions were reportedly in his hands at least twenty-four hours before the coup; he allegedly was led to believe that the coup was scheduled for some time later in the year.[6] As minister of interior, with concomitant security responsibilities, Pazhwak was in a good position both to warn Daoud that his conspirators' identities and plans had been compromised, as well as to mislead Abdul Wali as to the date of the probable coup.

With this kind of leftist involvement, there is no doubt that the Soviets were at least aware of Daoud's plans in advance, if indeed they did not actively promote them for their own purposes. There would have been every reason for them to assist him in seizing power.

In Mohammed Daoud they had a prospective figurehead chief of state whose noncommunist credentials were impeccable: as a first cousin of the monarch he wished to depose, and as a former prime minister who had demonstrated his true nonalignment by encouraging both Soviet and American aid, Daoud would scarcely call forth any strong American objection if he took over. At the same time, the opportunities for Soviet influence in Afghan affairs would be strengthened immeasurably by the coterie of Parchamis and Khalqis surrounding him. Not only might they influence Afghan policies in directions favorable to Soviet interests, but it could be done without any Soviet ideological commitment or responsibility for the actions of the "noncommunist" Afghan government.

This factor was especially important for the Soviets in relation to the Pashtunistan issue. Ever since Daoud left power in 1963, the Afghan monarchy had made consistent efforts to downplay Pashtunistan and to keep relations with Pakistan as cordial as possible. In 1973, with the re-formation of the former East and West Pakistans into Bangladesh and Pakistan, respectively, there was a clear opportunity for further weakening the already somewhat insecure government in Islamabad.[7]

From the Soviet standpoint, to ignore such a potential would be to miss an opportunity to undermine a friend of China and an ally of the United States. At the same time, the Soviet Union had to play a delicate game in this regard, for it did not wish to offend other Islamic states with which it had good relations. In Daoud, the USSR had a proxy for helping to destabilize Pakistan without the USSR having to take responsibility for such activity. Daoud's own well-known dedication to Pashtunistan would be enough to mask any Soviet involvement.

A somewhat similar situation existed with respect to Iran. The Shafiq government had reached an agreement with Iran over allocation of the Helmand River waters so necessary for irrigating both Afghan and Iranian territory. Some Afghans, supported if not led and inspired by Parcham and Khalq, insisted that the monarchy had sold out Afghan water rights to the Iranians. At the same time, the fact that some Baluchi tribesmen (included as part of the Pashtunistan issue) inhabited southeastern Iran automatically extended that problem into Iranian territory. Again, the USSR had every motive for embarrassing a U.S. ally (Iran being at that time the strongest bulwark of anticommunist defense in the Middle East) without itself taking responsibility for hurting an Islamic power.

Finally, regardless of the results inside Iran or Pakistan, abrasive Afghan behavior could be counted on to alienate Afghanistan from the West and by default drive it into a closer relationship with the USSR.

The need for action from the Soviet standpoint was immediate. Ever since the 1969 elections, and especially since the Shafiq government's crackdown on dissidents, leftist strength (although occasionally showing itself in student demonstrations and strikes) had been waning.[8] By contrast, Western influence, despite a fall-off in U.S. government aid, appeared to be growing. The establishment of a Western-sponsored Industrial Development Bank of Afghanistan in March 1973, for example, was designed to allow a multinational bank consortium from France, Britain, the United States, and Japan to take on a 40 percent interest in development in the country. (The other 60 percent was to be in Afghan hands.)

Worse from the Soviet view, former Prime Minister Maiwandwal was building an ever more organized political party of his own, the Progressive Democratic Party (PDP), which was not at all in line with Soviet interests. The PDP envisaged creation of a firmly Islamic constitutional monarchy in Afghanistan, one that would evolve progressively into a social democracy after building a strong nationalist pan-Afghan ethos.[9]

Worst of all, Maiwandwal, along with forty-five noncommunist military officers, had been planning his own coup d'état against the Shafiq government. The timing for this is not known, but presumably it would have occurred later in 1973 if Daoud had not struck first. When Daoud's coup came, Maiwandwal was in Iraq on the last leg of a journey that had included stops in Moscow and Western Europe. While in Moscow he apparently sounded out Soviet leaders on what their reactions would be if the PDP were to come to power legally in the elections that were scheduled for that August and September. The Soviet reply was equivocal.[10] Given the state of Soviet espionage in Afghanistan, it is not unlikely that the Kremlin was aware of his coup plans as well. If so, there was good reason for the Soviets to prompt their adherents in Daoud's entourage to move ahead with dispatch to preempt the coup option.

For in Maiwandwal the Soviets must have recognized a threat to their long-term plans in Afghanistan. Even after Daoud succeeded, that threat remained. Not only was Maiwandwal a politically popular figure in Afghanistan as well as abroad, but his relations with Daoud and Naim were excellent. He had been Naim's protégé in the Foreign Ministry, and there was speculation that Daoud would groom him as a successor to his own leadership role. He would have been a powerful figure in any democratic government, and he thus represented a threat to the left.[11]

On return to Kabul from his trip, Maiwandwal held several long conversations with the two brothers, and his political future seemed bright. Within days, however, he was under arrest for allegedly plotting against the new regime, along with his previous coconspirators against the Shafiq government. Although there were reports that he had tried to dissuade his colleagues from taking any action against Daoud's government on the grounds that it deserved a chance to prove itself, tape recordings of purported conversations between him and the other conspirators were played for Daoud and convinced him of Maiwandwal's guilt. Maiwandwal was held incommunicado for several months, and then strangled in his cell by two "extreme leftists" on the night of October 20, 1973. Supposedly neither Daoud nor Naim had desired any harm to come to Maiwandwal, but they authorized the official cover-up story that he had committed suicide. Furthermore, Maiwandwal was later sentenced to death in absentia by the court that tried his colleagues.[12]

With Maiwandwal safely neutralized within days after the coup, the USSR could be forgiven for looking with some complacency on the Afghan situation. There was a predominance of leftists in the Daoud cabinet; a leftist-dominated Central Committee was giving advice behind the scenes; a group of leftist military officers was taking over the key military positions; and the Ministry of Interior (especially its police element) had been significantly penetrated by young Parchami officers.

The Soviets, however, had reckoned without the political acumen of the supposed figurehead, Sardar Mohammed Daoud.

Daoud's first move was to dissipate the dangerous concentration of Parchamis in the Ministry of Interior. Although the minister himself, Pazhwak, had been a valuable asset in the coup, he was transferred immediately to the politically less important position of minister of education. Daoud then broke up the Parchami nucleus by sending all 160 of them out into the Afghan rural districts with instructions to promote their progressive theories at the grassroots level.[13]

Although some Afghans were worried at the time that this move proved Daoud's leftist orientation and represented a genuine effort by him to spread Marxism, the reverse was almost certainly the case. Daoud understood his countrymen and the impossibility of altering traditional patterns of country life without applying Draconian methods. These methods he withheld from the young Parchamis, whose efforts to breach the "mud curtain" of rural Afghanistan were thus doomed to failure. Out of communication with each other and with the capital, they ceased to exist as a potential political force. Those who quit their posts and tried to return to Kabul were dealt with severely, losing their jobs (and sometimes even their freedom) for dereliction of duty.

Daoud's next move was more cautious and deliberate, but it was certainly unwelcome from the leftist viewpoint. Several months after taking power, he began reappointing his leftist ministers to new, less important positions. Daoud himself personally held the vital portfolios of Defense and Foreign Affairs, but leftists controlled a significant portion of the rest of his cabinet.

First to go was Pacha Gul Wafadar, an air force engineer who had been trained in the USSR, and who in March 1974 was relieved of his duties as minister of frontier and tribal affairs (a somewhat sensitive post in view of the Pashtunistan issue). He was posted with honor as ambassador to Bulgaria, but the "true" story of the transfer was leaked by the government and soon became common knowledge. He had secretly married a Soviet girl while in training in the USSR, and after the coup, he had brought her back to Afghanistan on the assumption that the old regulations prohibiting such liaisons had died with the monarchy. Daoud's punishment was to transfer him out of the country. The fact that he was a leftist ostensibly had no bearing on the matter.

Next, in April 1974 Abdul Hamid Mohtat, minister of communications, was dismissed abruptly. Like Pacha Gul Wafadar, he had been a member of the Central Committee as well as a minister. Unlike the latter, when he was fired from the ministry he lost his Central Committee membership as well, and received no other appointment. The reason for his expulsion was his failure to "follow the policy of the State and the fundamentals of the Central Committee," a charge no more enlightening today than it was in 1974.[14] The fact that Mohtat was posted as ambassador to Japan by both Khalq and Parcham communist governments does, however, offer implicit evidence that his allegiances have been consistently Marxist-Leninist.

In December 1974, Pazhwak was dismissed as minister of education, and nine months later, in September 1975, Daoud downgraded Faiz Mohammed from the key post of minister of interior to minister of frontier and tribal affairs, while at the same time he dismissed Ghulam Jailani Bakhtari as minister of agriculture. As if fearing that such humiliation of two leftists at once might arouse Soviet ire, Daoud simultaneously raised Minister of Finance Sayyid Abdulellah's status to that of second deputy prime minister.[15]

By early 1977, Abdulellah was the only man left in Daoud's cabinet with any known history of Parcham connections, although Minister of Commerce Mohammed Khan Jalalar (who was to receive the same portfolio under Babrak in 1980) was even then suspected by many Afghans of being secretly in league with the Soviets.[16] Faiz Mohammed had been posted as ambassador to Indonesia in September 1976, and in 1977 Hassan Sharq—the last of the well-known leftists—went to Japan in the same capacity.

If Daoud had moved swiftly against the young Parchamis in the Ministry of Interior and cautiously against his own leftist ministers, he was doubly cautious when it came to the military. This was where the real political power of the country lay and Daoud could not afford to offend any group within it. At the same time, it had been Daoud who, in his earlier term of office, had given the military the prestige that it enjoyed in 1973, and he appears to have believed that the key officers owed true allegiance to him. This belief was to prove a fatal error on his part in 1978.

Before that time, however, he appears to have entertained doubts about the loyalty of specific individuals in sensitive positions. For example, Captain Zia Mohammedzai Zia, commander of the Republican Guard, an elite detachment responsible for protecting the prime minister and other ranking government figures, was a well-known Parchami. Despite his modest rank, Zia commanded about two thousand highly trained troops who held the power of life and death over those whom they were supposed to protect. In 1975, Daoud promoted Zia to major, and then at the end of that year to lieutenant colonel—but simultaneously he posted him to New Delhi as military attaché. Zia was replaced by a lower-ranking but thoroughly loyal officer, Sahib Jan.

Another officer removed from a strategic post was Lieutenant Colonel Abdul Qader, who had led the air force in support of Daoud in 1973. At first appointed chief of staff for the air force, he was demoted and transferred for public criticism of Daoud. (He was restored to his former post in 1977.)[17]

The other officers were mostly left in place, including Captain (later Major) Mohammed Aslam Watanjar (who had commanded a key armored force in support of Daoud), Captain Sayed Mohammed Gulabzoy, and Major Shah Jan Mazdooryar. Like Qader, each of these three had received training in the USSR, each was to command troops against Daoud in 1978, and each was to receive a ministerial post in Taraki's communist government as a reward.[18] As long as such key leftist military figures remained in place, the USSR could feel (with good reason) that its ultimate interests in the country were being protected. With Daoud's one-man rule in effect, his departure from the scene for any reason—a coup led by the right or left, or merely the toll of his years—would leave the field open for a takeover by pro-Soviet elements in the army. The Maoist dictum that political power grows from gun barrels was and is a stark reality in a country with political institutions as underdeveloped as those in Afghanistan. This is a fact likely to be appreciated by those who, like the Soviets, saw their own immediate political forebears rise to power by force of arms.

Meanwhile, in the international arena, Daoud was taking a series of steps that were not in line with Soviet objectives. Initially, in 1973–74,

he reverted to traditionally aggressive Afghan policies on Pashtunistan. This, as has been noted, was fully in line with Soviet policies
designed to disrupt and destabilize Pakistan, especially now that the
latter was emerging as one of China's new allies.

By early 1975, however, Kabul was making quiet overtures to Islamabad to defuse the problem. These efforts continued for over a year
before they culminated, in the summer of 1976, in exchange visits
between presidents Ali Bhutto and Mohammed Daoud. A Pakistani
gesture that helped mollify Afghan public opinion was the offer of
generous aid to alleviate suffering caused by a severe earthquake and
floods in northern Afghanistan in early 1976. By August 31, 1976
(Pashtunistan Day in Afghanistan), relations had improved to such a
degree that this traditional occasion for inflammatory anti-Pakistan
agitation and propaganda passed in Kabul almost without public
notice.[19]

Of equal concern to Moscow must have been Afghanistan's rapprochement with Iran. In July 1974, a year after the coup, Afghanistan
signed a new development agreement under which Iran would finance
transportation and industrial projects whose total value was then estimated at $1 billion.[20] Later, the shah was to promise Afghanistan $2
billion for its Seven Year Plan. This was more than the total aid
proffered by all foreign donors since World War II,[21] though falling oil
revenues may have caused the Iranians subsequently to back off on this
commitment to some degree.[22] Whatever hopes the USSR might have
had for reaping political benefits from its own continuing economic aid
would have been dissipated if the Iranian projects had all gone forward. Few of them did, however, and most of the promised aid
remained unrealized. It was inordinately difficult for Iranians and
Afghans to reach agreement on projects during this period. One won-
ders whether the USSR was actively involved in trying to sabotage
them. With Jalalar as minister of commerce and Abdulellah as minister
of finance, there may have been opportunities for complicating negotiations; if so, it is hard to believe that they would have been overlooked.

Even without Iranian investments, Afghanistan was diversifying its
requests for aid in other directions. Saudi Arabia, India, and China
were among those countries that responded, and the influence of
Soviet aid projects dropped proportionately.

Taken in sum, all of the foregoing developments ran counter to

Moscow's interests. Even the Afghan political vulnerability to future coups, ensured by the one-man nature of Daoud's rule, appeared to be diminishing. In January 1977, after a year of quiet preparatory work, a constitutional commission presented its findings to a *loyah jirgah*. This was the first representative assembly convened since Daoud's assumption of power for the second time. Three weeks of substantive and vigorous debate on the commission's draft document produced a constitution that appeared to fit Afghanistan's needs.[23] An optimist could have looked forward to the development of a stable nation-state with a growing immunity to violent overthrow.

Although Soviet official propaganda still avoided criticism of the Daoud regime, Soviet displeasure with Afghanistan's policies was displayed in January 1977 during a trip by Daoud and Naim to Moscow. In a brief, hostile exchange, Brezhnev suddenly challenged Daoud to "get rid of all those imperialist advisors in your country." Daoud replied coldly that when Afghanistan had no further need of foreign advisors, they would *all* be asked to leave. Naim ascribed more significance to this exchange than did Daoud, who took it as nothing more than a typical Soviet gambit, designed to put him on the defensive.[24]

In early summer of 1977, the Khalq and Parcham factions of the old PDPA were officially reconciled and a new PDPA organization was formed.[25] The significance of this reunification, temporary as it turned out to be, is hard to overestimate, yet it went largely unnoticed (or was reported in distorted form) by Western students of Afghanistan until after the 1978 coup. While there is and can be no absolute proof of Soviet involvement in the rapprochement, the intensity of the Khalq-Parcham rivalry was always such that it is hard to conceive of the two parties having reached an agreement without outside pressure. Though such temporary accommodation between rival factions is not unusual in the West, the Afghan tradition of sworn enmity is one of the strongest in the whole culture. Only the application of some overriding force is likely to submerge such personal animosities as those existing between Babrak and Taraki. The implication is that the USSR stepped in to heal the breach, and that serious, detailed coup plotting—with or without immediate Soviet guidance—can be dated from that event.

Through the balance of 1977, Daoud appeared to be relying ever more heavily on a small inner cabinet of advisors who seemed to have replaced the former, pro-Soviet Central Committee. The only member of this group who had any record of association with Parcham was Abdulellah. Only in April 1978, days before his death, did Daoud seem to be ready to open up the advisory group to a wider spectrum of political thought and technical expertise, even reviving the name Central Committee. By then it was too late.[26]

In the meantime, a series of apparently political assassinations had occurred in Kabul. In August 1977 a pilot of the Afghan national airlines (Ariana), who had been instrumental in leading a successful strike, was shot to death outside his apartment. The pilot resembled Babrak and was his neighbor, leading to speculation that he might have been a victim of mistaken identity. In November, the apparently apolitical minister of planning, Ahmad Ali Khoram, was marched at gunpoint by a solitary assassin from his office to a public square where he was killed. The killer confessed under torture to having fifty-four colleagues who were allegedly involved in a plot to assassinate Daoud and his cabinet. The government said that he had been trained outside Afghanistan, but provided no further details.[27] These killings have not been solved, and it is questionable whether either one really was political.

The final assassination, however, became political whether or not it was originally intended to be so. On the night of April 17, 1978, Mir Akbar Khyber, a well-known Parcham idealogue and one of the founding editors of *Parcham*, was murdered by persons still unknown. Two days later, the PDPA, blaming that assassination on the CIA, staged a surprisingly large demonstration of some ten to fifteen thousand marchers for Khyber's funeral.[28] Daoud moved swiftly to arrest leading leftists, but his actions were not decisive enough: there was no concerted move against leftist military officers and Hafizullah Amin, the pivotal Khalqi organizer of military cadres, was held under only very loose house arrest for a critical ten-and-a-half-hour period at the start of the police sweep.

These tactical errors were to cost Daoud his life within the next twenty-four hours, and ultimately, they cost Afghanistan its national independence. One must question how much longer the Soviets would have allowed Daoud and his regime to survive anyway. By 1977 the USSR must have realized that he could not be manipulated, and from then on it was just a matter of time before they took steps to establish a government more amenable to Soviet aims and control.

In giving up its effort at covert manipulation, however, the USSR had to pay a price. Although the PDPA stoutly affirmed its nationalist and independent nonalignment, that line was difficult to put across convincingly. The PDPA's Marxist-Leninist orientation was too well known, and Soviet intentions toward the country were emerging ever more obviously, in spite of continuing efforts to mask them.

CHAPTER
7

The Drive for
Political Control: 3
Rule by Communist Party Proxy
May 1978–August 1979

To the foreign observer who is not directly aiding a coup conspiracy, the coup itself almost always comes as a surprise. It can scarcely be otherwise, for if a disinterested outsider is aware of the plotting, so in all likelihood are the security organs of the regime that hopes to stay in power. Coups, therefore, must be designed in secret, with knowledge of the full plan restricted to the smallest possible group of leaders, individual details portioned out carefully only to those with the most essential need to know, and the one vital detail, the timing, held secret until the last possible moment.

Thus it usually requires time for most foreign governments to react to the fact of a coup and to assess the survival potential of the new government before rushing to extend recognition. In 1978, as in 1973, the first country to recognize the new Afghan government was the USSR. The suspicion that the Soviets had foreknowledge of the 1978 coup is heightened by the fact that Soviet recognition came on Sunday, April 30, in the middle of the long weekend celebrations for May Day. Interestingly, the announcement came first from Kabul, and was still unconfirmed in Moscow on May 1.[1]

The 1978 coup had several unusual aspects. The first was the PDPA claim that it drilled its military members beforehand in their duties with great thoroughness, holding some ten rehearsals! It was able to run such drills without compromise because it camouflaged them (by means that have not been spelled out openly) so that "had Daoud been intimated (sic) he would not have suspected any of the measures against his regime."[2] Whatever the cover, it was clearly adequate and the drills were an essential element of success for the small group of Afghan officers who had to act decisively and in concert to overcome the disadvantage of their numbers.

A second unusual aspect was Taraki's specific instruction concerning events that should be considered as adequate reason for triggering the coup:

> Should imperialism, reaction, or another group topple the Daoud Regime, the Democratic People's Party of Afghanistan should wrest the political power. In case the Daoud regime launched an offensive to incarcerate me (Comrade Taraki) in order to weaken or destroy the party members, the latter should commence the revolution to topple the Daoud Regime and wrest the political power.[3]

If this quote, unfortunately undated, was not made up after the fact, it provides a curiously specific set of circumstances—and only two of them at that—for "wresting the political power." It is almost as if Taraki had reason to anticipate a real or sham right-wing coup or his own arrest.

In this regard, another circumstance is even more significant. After the popular demonstrations that followed Mir Akbar Khyber's assassination, the midnight police sweep that resulted in Taraki's arrest and immediate incarceration also included the arrest of Amin and three other (unnamed) members of the PDPA Central Committee. Whereas Taraki was taken straight to jail, however, Amin was held under very loose house arrest for more than ten hours, from midnight to 10:45 A.M. on April 26. During this critical period he received visitors, sent his sons out to get information and to contact his Khalqi recruits in the military, and dispatched instructions to the latter on what each was to do—all without more than passing hindrance by his guards.

Finally (in the words of the PDPA), "At 10:30 A.M. on the twenty-sixth of April, work on planning and the revolution command was finalized and at 10:45 of the same day, three cars with armed policemen carried Comrade Amin to the jail, where he was delivered at exactly 11 A.M."[4]

Taraki had delegated to Amin the task of recruiting military officers into Khalq as early as 1973.[5] Of all the individuals for Daoud to have left essentially at large when a left wing upheaval threatened, Amin was without doubt the most dangerous. The explanation for this fatal laxness may lie in the allegation by one analyst that the third in command (unnamed) of Daoud's primary intelligence unit was a Khalqi "mole."[6] Any such person would doubtless have had advance warning of the arrests and might have had enough influence to arrange for a delay in Amin's removal to jail.

Or did the USSR have its own "moles" who helped to sabotage Daoud's arrest order and to coordinate the PDPA activities after arrests began cutting into PDPA ranks? Persistent reports of unusual activity at the Soviet Embassy in Kabul during the period of the coup are not proof of such involvement,[7] but do tend to discount Soviet Ambassador Puzanov's ingenuous statement, "no one was more surprised than I by the coup."[8]

As in 1973, there can be little doubt that the USSR was at least aware of the conspirators' coup plans; many of the Afghans were the same individuals who brought Daoud to power. The intention, however, had been to act somewhat later, in August, as eventually stated by Taraki himself.[9] The coup was close to fruition anyway and only needed to be launched a few months earlier than originally anticipated.

An intriguing question is whether the triggering catalyst for the coup—Khyber's assassination—was a part of anyone's plans. From the Soviet and Parcham standpoint it surely was not, and to that extent Puzanov's statement can be taken at face value: he very likely expected events to unfold as they did, but in August, not April. Whether the Khalqis were caught unaware is less certain. In any case, it is interesting that almost from the outset of Taraki's rule the fact of Khyber's murder and its significance for the coup were ignored completely. The first full official report of the coup by the Taraki government does not even mention Khyber or the demonstrations surrounding his funeral march. Daoud's roundup of leftists is portrayed as an unprovoked police action.[10]

To the outside world, the coup came as a shock. Preliminary analysis in the West gave a picture of a beleaguered Afghan Left that staked all on a final, desperate throw of the dice to unseat Daoud. In the chaotic situation that developed, both loyalist and rebel forces made multiple errors and "the side with the fewer foul-ups won."[11]

In fact, however, there were remarkably few foul-ups on the part of the PDPA. Though extensive, PDPA penetrations of the military comprised only a small fraction of the officer corps, and though all of the party leadership had been in jail since the twenty-sixth, the military penetrations acted with surprisingly good coordination. Amin's written instructions to them, composed and delivered between midnight and early morning of the twenty-sixth, provided a point of departure but were scarcely a substitute for ongoing leadership and command. By the time action commenced, on the morning of the twenty-seventh, the PDPA military officers were apparently on their own.

Amin's instructions had reportedly reached their recipients in *photocopy* form.[12] Bearing in mind that one can scarcely obtain photocopies commercially in Kabul in the best of circumstances, much less in the dawn hours, the implication is that diplomatic copying facilities were warmed up and waiting. Major Sayed Mohammed Gulabzoy, the individual responsible for delivering the instructions, had, as will be seen, close Soviet ties and would have known where to turn.[13] He appears to have served in a coordination, if not command, capacity once Amin was in jail.

Although there were communications failures and reported instances of inadvertent engagements between friendly forces, they were virtually unavoidable, for both sides used the same equipment and wore the same uniforms. It was safer for each individual to shoot first rather than wait for proper identification of friends or enemies.

The PDPA appeared to have penetrations in no fewer than twenty military units and airports.[14] Some of their officers were in key command positions; these included Majors Aslam Watanjar, Shah Jan Mazdooryar, and Assadullah Payam in the Fourth Armored Division; and Lieutenant Colonel Abdul Qader who was chief of staff of the air force. Others held secondary ranks but were able to kill or incapacitate the pro-Daoud commanders and take charge themselves. This happened in the Thirty-Second Brigade, the Eighty-Eighth Antiaircraft Artillery Unit, and in the Commandos. In the Seventh Division, the would-be PDPA commander, Mohammed Ali, was himself killed.[15]

The Republican Guard, the Fifteenth Armored Division, and the Seventh Division remained loyal and fought on behalf of Daoud. By the early morning hours of April 28, however, only the remnants of the Republican Guard still held out. It was the one unit that apparently had no reliable surviving PDPA penetrations. Until heavy losses forced surrender, it continued to defend the presidential palace where

Daoud, his immediate family, and some close advisors had taken refuge.

They were all gathered in one room when a PDPA officer entered and demanded that Daoud surrender unconditionally. Instead, Daoud drew his pistol and opened fire. Others followed suit, and in the brief firefight that followed, Daoud and almost all of his family—including ten women and several children, the youngest of whom was three years old—were slain.[16]

The reign of the Mohammedzai family, extending almost unbroken back to the early nineteenth century, had ended; the long-term Soviet goal of establishing a pliable regime in Kabul had apparently been achieved.

On the part of both the Soviet Union and the Kabul regime, however, there was a concentrated and partially successful effort to deny the fact that Afghanistan was now committed to the Soviet Bloc. This effort was to continue into 1979, despite overwhelming evidence to the contrary, but it was particularly intense in the first days following the coup.[17] To describe the regime, terms such as "democratic, Islamic, reformist, and nonaligned,"[18] "progressive and patriotic,"[19] and (most hoary of all) "agrarian reformers"[20] were used by Afghan authorities, independent journalists, and even some Western students of the area who should have known better.

Another effort to downplay the significance of the coup was apparent in the deliberate Afghan understatement of casualties. Although the first Western reports almost surely exaggerated the bloodshed (initial reports were of ten thousand killed), the deaths unquestionably were in the thousands, not the "under one hundred" initially claimed by Taraki.[21] The two-thousand-strong Republican Guard, for example, fought until there were only some two hundred of them left, and when they finally surrendered, most were shot out-of-hand. A few were sent to Pul-e-Charki jail, but most of that group were also killed during the next few months in nightly executions by firing squad.[22]

Nonetheless, initial Afghan and Soviet propaganda was designed to convey the impression that the coup was a purely local phenomenon, an almost unopposed removal of a hated tyrant by a popular uprising that owed nothing to outside influence.

While that picture is obviously distorted, the extent of Soviet influence is extremely difficult to measure, due to the secretiveness of both Afghan and Soviet sources. In the first months following the coup,

Soviet influence did not amount to complete control, or the Parcham/ Khalq conflict would not have been allowed to split the PDPA anew. On the other hand, it was pervasive, as indicated by an oblique reference made by Taraki to the Central Committee Historical Commission in November 1978. Following a description of the organization of party commissions and duties of party secretaries in managing state and party affairs, he said,

> This has been organized on the basis of profound studies and specialized advices [sic]. During the first days of the Revolution some persons who had specialization in Party organization came to Kabul at the invitation of the Secretariat of the Party and studied for three months Party affairs here and consequently they gave specialized advice to the Party and it was on the basis of these advices that the Party is always organized.[23]

While Taraki did not name the nationality of the advisors, there can be little doubt that they came from the USSR. The task apparently was to help the PDPA in the difficult transition stage from its role as a conspiratorial underground opposition to that of a ruling party.

In the first PDPA cabinet, announced on May 1, 1978, the strength of Parcham and Khalq seemed to have been carefully balanced by assigning ministries in order of importance first to one faction and then to the other. In fact, although the Khalqis held the nominally top positions of prime minister (Nur Mohammed Taraki) and minister of foreign affairs (Hafizullah Amin), Parcham appeared to control the ministries of defense, interior, and communications. Of these latter, the ministry of defense is the ultimate source of political power in the country, while the ministries of interior and communications have high strategic importance as well. Inasmuch as Parcham had always had the reputation of being slightly favored over Khalq by the Soviets, the apparent Parcham upper hand was not surprising.

The Parchami minister of defense, Abdul Qader, however, though a hero of the revolution, was no politician. As noted above, he had helped Daoud come to power in 1973, and had been elevated to the position of air force chief of staff; but he then had criticized Daoud for moving too slowly toward socialism, and had been demoted promptly to officer in charge of military slaughterhouses. Later reinstated to his former position by Daoud, he led the air force against his mentor, playing a key role in the 1978 coup.[24]

The PDPA figure who had the closest connections with the military was the Khalqi Hafizullah Amin. It was he who had recruited most of the military cadres for Khalq, and who had done the organizational work for the coup among the military. He was also a politician at heart, and would not have been likely to relinquish his military contacts after the coup had succeeded. In fact, on being released from jail the evening of April 27, "Comrade Amin introduced other Central Committee members to the revolutionary officers."[25] The implication is that up until that time, both Khalqi and Parchami penetrations of the military had been compartmented even from other Central Committee members, who had communicated with them only through Amin. Thus, though Parcham was also represented in the military, and a Parchami was minister of defense, it is probable that Khalq had the dominant influence in the armed forces.

Furthermore, although the ministry of interior was in the hands of a loyal Parchami (Nur Ahmad Nur), the reputedly Parchami-oriented minister of communications (Aslam Watanjar) successfully converted to Khalq when the Parchamis were purged.

Through May and the first week in June, there were few outward manifestations of the struggle for control of the PDPA that must have been going on between Khalqis and Parchamis. In the pages of the *Kabul Times*, pictures of Parcham leaders appeared as often as those of Khalqis. On May 22, however, the Political Department of the Armed Forces of Afghanistan published a pamphlet ("On the Saur Revolution") that avoided all mention of such Parcham figures as Babrak and Anahita Ratebzad, although it paid due respect to such pro-Parcham military officers as Qader. (The effusive praise heaped on Amin in this publication was a good indication of the influence that he continued to wield in the military.)

In the middle of June, there was, in the *Kabul Times*, a sudden cessation of photos of PDPA leaders, Parcham and Khalq alike. The last photo before this blackout was on June 8, when Babrak was featured warmly welcoming Amin back from a visit abroad. In late June, pictures of Amin and Taraki began to appear again—at the same time that foreign postings of ranking Parchamis also began to be announced.

Although Khalq thus declared subtly that it had won the first round for control of the party, the struggle itself appeared to have been conducted in a relatively civilized manner. The losers, in line with precommunist Afghan tradition, were sent abroad into honorable, ambassadorial exile.

Following the announcement of the departure of the principal Parchamis in early July, the personality cult that had been building up around Taraki ever since the coup became more apparent, recalling the days of Stalin. On July 25 he was referred to as "Great Leader" in the *Kabul Times,* and this sobriquet soon appeared in almost every news story that mentioned his name—a large percentage of the stories printed at that time. Virtually every indoors photograph showing any Afghan official other than Taraki himself managed to include in it a portrait of Great Leader. (The definite article was usually omitted in the headlines, lending an even more Stalinist aspect to the coverage.)

By early August the portraits on the wall (obviously dubbed into the photographs) were dwarfing the ministers conducting business under their benign gaze.[26] The portraits also tended to be more in focus than the faces of the ministers, which over time seemed to become ever smaller and more fuzzily anonymous.

On August 17, the regime announced the arrest of General Abdul Qader for plotting against it.[27] Other arrests followed, including that of the ministers of public works (Lt. Col. Mohammed Rafiee) and of planning (Sultan Ali Kishtmand). Only a month later did the extent of the purported plot emerge, as the government newspapers devoted entire over-size editions on September 23 to the confessions of the conspirators.[28]

The Afghan media were at first apparently hesitant to heap too much ideological abuse on Babrak and the other exiled Parchamis who were also implicated in the conspiracy. The plotters reportedly intended to follow the same foreign and domestic policies as the existing regime, but under a renamed *People's* Democratic Republic of Afghanistan. Relying on "national progressive forces," the conspirators promised to share power with the Khalqis if the latter would agree to cooperate. The coup was scheduled for August, during the Eid festival that marks the end of the Ramadan fast. (This was, by the way, the time originally set by the PDPA for the coup against Daoud.) The Parchamis abroad would return to Kabul unannounced via Iran and Pakistan to lead the coup. The motive for the coup was given as the frustrated personal ambitions of Babrak and others who had been shunted aside by the Khalqis.[29]

All of this is fairly straightforward and probably accurate. What is far harder to clarify are murky allegations by the Afghan press concerning the involvement of foreign powers in the plot. Evidence for such involvement was claimed "on the basis of undeniable documents" yet nowhere is there a hint of the countries involved. The foreign linkage was allegedly via unspecified "elements attached to reaction and imperialism"[30]—yet the foreign powers were said also to have a "political accord" with the plotters that the latter should continue the Afghan policy of "positive and active nonalignment"—a standard euphemism for an ostensibly neutral but firmly pro-Soviet orientation.

It seemed bizarre at the time that the USSR might be involved in toppling the regime of its own client state, a hypothesis that only became undeniably credible when, fifteen months later, Babrak was returned to power by an invading Soviet army. Nevertheless, even in 1978 the USSR had reason to be dismayed with the course of events in Afghanistan. Worse, from the Kremlin's standpoint, its power to dictate corrective measures to the regime in power was circumscribed to some degree.

As long as Parcham and Khalq had been in quasi-legal opposition to the Afghan government, the USSR had had leverage to force them into mending their differences. Once the reunited PDPA succeeded in "wresting the political power" from Daoud in April 1978, however, it gained a greater measure of independence from the USSR, especially in the conduct of its internal affairs. Inasmuch as both Khalq and Parcham factions were apparently equally pro-Soviet, Moscow at first seems to have assumed that it did not matter very much which faction emerged victorious in their own internal struggle. There was probably some hope that the two in fact could reach a lasting compromise, and if they could not, Moscow was then prepared to go along with whichever faction triumphed. A few leaders might be deposed, jailed, or even executed, but in the end the party would emerge the stronger for having purged itself of leadership elements personally unable to accommodate to the winners.

What the USSR overlooked (and apparently has continued to overlook) is the depth of hostility that Afghan enemies (especially Pashtuns) develop against each other as a matter of course. The term *feudal* has a meaning that extends beyond economics, and Afghanistan is especially feudal when it comes to loyalties and antagonisms. The Pashtunwali, the Pashtun code of conduct, which tradition demands be memorized by all Pashtun youths, sets forth the rules governing blood feuds as a first order of business. Such feuds know no bounds in time or space, and the exacting of vengeance is supposed to be a priority matter for every wronged individual or (if he is killed) for his appropriate surviving male relative, whether or not the latter was personally wronged.

The hostilities that developed between Parcham and Khalq from 1967 to 1977 were far too fundamental to be reconciled by one year of enforced cooperation. The antagonism did not exist merely at the top level, but extended down to the rank and file as well. No matter that the two factions, even when combined, were still only a tiny minority of the population (only a few thousand out of perhaps fifteen to seventeen million), and that excommunication of one or the other from the PDPA would imperil the very survival of the party. Vengeance was more important, and the Khalqis lost no time in exacting it. As soon as it became apparent that the Parcham leadership had lost in the struggle with Khalq, Parchamis at all levels were hounded, imprisoned, and often shot. (Had Parcham emerged the victor, there might have been somewhat less violent a reaction—Parcham was less Pashtun-oriented than Khalq, though it still had a significant Pashtun membership—but some degree of violence would have been inevitable. As experience in 1980 has shown, Khalqi losers are no less bloodthirsty than Khalqi winners, and the feud would have erupted in any case.)

Despite the still tenuous hold that Taraki had on the country, by eliminating the Parchamis he and his followers had cut their meager support by more than half. Furthermore, free of the somewhat moderating Parchami influence, the regime undertook policies that were ever less acceptable to the Afghan population at large. Daoud's exile of the 160 Parchami reformers into the countryside as sub-governors had given Parcham an education in rural realities not shared by Khalqi urban intellectuals. Having themselves tried—and failed—to impose reforms from above in the countryside, the Parchamis doubtless counseled caution to Khalqi colleagues, advice that was ignored once the Parchami leaders were deposed.

Khalqi insensitivity to public opinion continued to be illustrated after the Parcham coup failed. On October 19, after preliminary publicity that should have provided a chance for opponents to voice objections, Taraki personally raised Afghanistan's new national banner—a blood-red, close copy of the Soviet flag. His elimination of Islamic green from the national standard was one of the most foolish of his many provocative moves against Afghan tradition. In 1980, Babrak was to restore a version of the old flag in a belated and unsuccessful attempt to regain public confidence.

From the Soviet standpoint, Taraki's negative impact in the country-side was a serious matter. Immediately after the coup (and sporadically at later dates), the Kabul regime appeared to be trying to revive the Pashtunistan issue.[31] Even more than in the case of predecessor regimes, the USSR had reason for wishing Taraki success in this effort. With a firmly pro-Soviet regime in power in Kabul, instability to the south and west opened up ever greater opportunities for Soviet interference and ultimate control in those regions as well. Many in the West had forebodings of just such a development.[32]

Far from establishing a base for spreading unrest among Pashtuns on the other side of the border, however, Taraki's policies from the outset alienated his own Pashtun population to an ever greater extent. Rural resentment had already become resistance; resistance was becoming rebellion;[33] and rebellion showed signs of becoming a *jihad*, a holy war against the infidel Kabul regime. Instead of being an exporter of instability, Afghanistan showed signs of becoming an unwilling importer as refugees from the Khalqis flowed into Pakistan, established their own settlements, and set up lines of communication back into their homeland.

As a result of all this, the USSR had cause to support Babrak covertly in 1978, just as they would later, in 1979, support him openly with their armed forces. Babrak could be counted on to pursue more sophisticated, less abrasive policies toward the population than Taraki. On the other hand, in 1978 the Soviets were still attempting to preserve the fiction of their noninvolvement in Afghan internal affairs. Unless and until Babrak were securely in power in Kabul, the USSR would be risking serious embarrassment by aiding him; great pains would have been taken to conceal any such involvement.

If the USSR was in fact supporting Babrak, did the Khalqis detect that fact? It seems not, although as indicated above they appeared to be convinced that *some* foreign power was involved. In the days following the September 23 exposé, Kabul newspapers were more than usually effusive in praise for the USSR; they were also careful to replay Soviet praise for the Taraki regime.[34] At the same time however, at least one ranking bloc diplomat left Kabul under unexplained circumstances. Hermann Schwiessau, ambassador from the German Democratic Republic, presented his credentials on August 8, 1978, yet departed permanently and without any newspaper coverage some time during the next few months. He was to be replaced, probably in early 1979, by one Kraft Bumbel, whose arrival went similarly unannounced.

The Soviet ambassador, Puzanov, remained at his post. A year later, after involving himself more directly in Afghan internal politics, he was indeed asked to leave, but in 1978 there was no evidence of Afghan displeasure with him or his country.

Whether or not the USSR had tried to aid Babrak, it appeared to decide at this point to accommodate itself more thoroughly to the Khalqi regime. In fact, relations seemed to move ahead significantly. In November the Afghan ambassador in Moscow was quoted as having declared that Afghan-Soviet relations were now changing from friendship to fraternity. Challenged with defining the meaning of this change, Amin insisted that despite some parallels with Soviet policy Afghanistan was still following a "strict policy of nonalignment."[35] It was not a convincing statement.

At the same time, the USSR may have been successful in persuading Taraki to take a softer line internally. Although the decision on the new Soviet-style flag was not rescinded (it would have represented too sharp a retreat), in late October the regime released from jail seventy-three women and children belonging to the former ruling family.[36] They were given the option of remaining in Afghanistan and working for the new regime, or emigrating permanently. Inasmuch as their property and possessions had been confiscated, most chose to emigrate. Their release was a surprisingly lenient move for the hard-line Khalqis to make.

Perhaps even more surprising was the continued survival of General Abdul Qader and Sultan Ali Kishtmand. It is the practice of most communist states to mete out justice, especially capital punishment, without delay. Afghanistan has been no exception in this regard (nor was it before the communists took over, for that matter), yet Qader's death sentence for his part in the anti-Khalq conspiracy was never carried out. One can only assume that there was significant pressure from some quarter (most logically the USSR) to stay the execution. The following year, in October 1979, Amin commuted Qader's sentence to fifteen years imprisonment, possibly as a further placating gesture toward the USSR.

On December 3, 1978, the Afghans signed a Friendship Agreement with the USSR in Moscow. The provisions of the treaty, including

Article IV which stipulated that the signatories "shall consult with each other and take by agreement appropriate measures to ensure the security, independence, and territorial integrity of the two countries. . ." indeed signaled a closer relationship.[37] Furthermore, as noted by some Western observers, similar friendship treaties signed by India (1971) and Vietnam (1978) had been the immediate precursors of violent aggression by those two countries against their neighbors: India's invasion of East Pakistan (thereafter Bangladesh) and Vietnam's invasion of Cambodia.[38] While it seemed clear that Afghanistan at that time was not in a position to invade anybody, there was an obvious need for more Soviet arms and advisors just to keep the country from falling to the insurgents.

In February 1979 the abduction and murder of U.S. Ambassador Adolph Dubs in downtown Kabul appeared to demonstrate the Afghan authorities' inability, even when closely coached by Soviet monitors, to deal with antiregime violence. In fact, the circumstances surrounding the Dubs murder are still unclear, especially in regard to motive. The Afghans claim that the abductors were Muslim zealots who wished to force the liberation of their religious leaders being held by the regime. (It is unclear why they thought that in "socialist" Afghanistan the U.S. ambassador would be a more suitable hostage for this purpose than one from a Warsaw Pact country.) In the Soviet-directed shootout between Afghan police and the abductors that followed (unsuccessfully protested by American diplomats on the scene before it began), Ambassador Dubs and two of his captors died immediately. Two other captors were seen to be taken alive, but their dead bodies were displayed by the authorities later the same day.

Soviet propaganda has worked at spreading the concept that the CIA, in an obscure plot to cause a rupture in Afghan-American relations, was behind the abduction.[39] This motive is far more plausible if ascribed to the USSR, whose consistent interest in seeing Afghan ties with the West impaired was, if anything, heightened by the deteriorating security situation in the country. Furthermore, the death of a U.S. envoy at the hands of purported Muslim fanatics could be expected to dampen any U.S. enthusiasm for possible future support to Muslim rebels operating out of Pakistan, and thus indirectly to help Taraki preserve his regime. That it does not seem to have had either effect is no thanks to the USSR.

Meantime, Soviet arms continued to be delivered to Afghanistan, but without any appreciable effect on government success in stamping out rebel activities. Instead of intimidating the resistance, the new levels of Soviet military aid seemed to inflame it. In March 1979 the city of Herat in western Afghanistan was engulfed by a spontaneous rebellion that saw some forty Soviet advisors and dependents massacred by the population. Overall Soviet deaths in clashes with insurgents were estimated at one hundred for the month.[40]

Possibly in response to this heightened violence, Taraki turned over the position of premier to Amin at the end of March. Taraki retained the positions of both defense minister and head of state, but Amin's new authority was thought to herald both firmer measures against the Muslim insurgents and closer Afghan ties to Moscow. Amin was believed to be "a hardline communist . . . even more servile to the Soviet Union than President Taraki."[41] At the same time, Soviet arms aid to Afghanistan was reported to have increased.[42]

The arms aid was followed immediately by a visit to Afghanistan by a Soviet military team headed by General Aleksey Alekseyevich Yepishev. Yepishev, who had played a major role in the 1968 Soviet occupation of Czechoslovakia, was one of the highest ranking Soviet officers to go to Afghanistan, and his visit was taken as a reflection of the seriousness of the problems facing the Afghan army in attempting to put down the Muslim insurgents.[43]

Although the news took months to seep out to the West, Yepishev's visit coincided with the deliberate massacre of the entire male population of the village of Kerala, northeast of Kabul, where over eleven hundred people were shot by Afghan troops and police under the direct command of Soviet advisors because the village was suspected (with good reason) of having supported the insurgents.[44] Far from discouraging the resistance, however, this mass execution seemed only to inflame it.

As the year advanced, the Kabul government's inability to deal with the insurgency became more and more apparent. In early August, a mutiny inside Kabul's Bala Hissar fortress had to be put down with helicopter gunships and tanks, in a battle that lasted for four hours.[45] A week later, an entire Afghan armored brigade went over to the insurgents taking its equipment with it.[46]

At this point Afghanistan received a visit by another prestigious Soviet military figure, General Ivan G. Pavlovskiy, commanding general of all Soviet ground forces. Pavlovskiy arrived in mid-August, with an entourage of fifty officers, and stayed for nearly two months.[47] His visit was not announced in the Kabul press and only later came to light in the West.[48]

In spite (or perhaps because) of the deteriorating security situation and the presence of a ranking Soviet general, President Taraki left on September 1 for the Non-Aligned Nations' Conference in Havana. His route, going and returning, lay via the USSR, and he stopped over briefly in Moscow on both legs of his journey. The details of his discussions there are a Kremlin secret, but it was credibly reported that the USSR successfully pressured him into reconciling his differences with Babrak and laying plans for a renewed Parcham-Khalq coalition government.[49] It was also reported that, while in Moscow, Taraki met with Babrak, to seal the bargain.[50]

To explain the sudden rehabilitation of Babrak, who had been excoriated in the Afghan press as a vile traitor, it was necessary to find some new villain whose alleged false witness had misled Taraki concerning Babrak. Such a scapegoat could also be held responsible for all else that had gone wrong in Afghanistan over the past eighteen months. The intended victim was Hafizullah Amin.[51]

It should have been abundantly clear to Moscow that even liquidation of Amin and a Parcham-Khalq reconciliation would not be sufficient to stem the insurgency. The only chance to pacify the country lay in Soviet military intervention. One can postulate, therefore, that Taraki returned to Afghanistan with a plan not only to denounce, arrest, and execute Amin (possibly on the grounds of the same accusation that was to appear later—that Amin was a CIA agent) and to effect a public reconciliation with Babrak, but also to announce jointly with him an invitation for active Soviet participation (i.e., combat troops) to dispose of the insurgency. Both the continued presence in Afghanistan of the large Pavlovskiy military delegation and a sudden upsurge in Soviet military activity near the Afghan border in mid-September lend credence to this hypothesis.[52]

Taraki returned to Kabul on September 11 and reported immediately to the Cabinet. During his absence, there had been no diminution of his personality cult in the Afghan media. From September 2 through September 12, the front page lead headline in every issue of the *Kabul Times* referred in one context or another to "Great Leader." On September 13, this practice suddenly came to a permanent halt.

September 14 was a Friday, the Muslim sabbath, so no newspaper appeared. The next (September 15) issue featured front page coverage of a news conference Taraki had held in Havana, but this clearly represented an *ad hoc* insertion of dated material by editors who must have been puzzled by the absence of copy on their most consistent news subject. By that time, unknown to any but Amin's inner circle, Taraki was already under arrest.

On September 16 all of Taraki's titles were assumed by Amin. Almost as a footnote, it was announced that the Plenum of the Central Committee had approved Taraki's request to be relieved of his duties "in view of my bad health and nervous weakness."[53]

On September 12, between Taraki's return and his "resignation," Amin had held a sudden press conference, in which he vigorously denied that the major military airbase at Bagram (near Kabul) had been turned over to the USSR, declared that Soviet troops were not involved in fighting insurgents and would not be so involved in the future, and asserted that Afghanistan had no intention of joining the Warsaw Pact.[54] Previous reports in the Western media had indeed claimed that such measures were being undertaken or were in the offing. Amin's denials were therefore not completely unprovoked. Nevertheless their timing and vehemence probably represent his first steps to thwart Taraki's plans to deliver the country into Soviet hands and make Amin a scapegoat.

Amin did not confine himself to words. On the same day as the press conference he quietly dismissed three key members of the Cabinet: Minister of Interior Watanjar (shifted six weeks earlier from his even more strategic position of minister of defense, which was assumed by Amin), Minister of Communications Gulabzoy, and Minister of Frontier Affairs Mazdooryar (former minister of interior who was shifted to frontier affairs when Watanjar took over interior).

All three of these men had been instrumental in bringing Daoud to power in 1973; all three had played key roles in the 1978 coup that toppled him; and all three, although originally Parchamis, had survived Babrak's downfall in 1978 by switching their allegiance to Khalq. Furthermore, all three were then to make yet another apparent reversal by rejoining Babrak as Cabinet members in January 1980, following the Soviet invasion. In the interim, despite protests by Amin and his foreign minister, Shah Wali, they were given asylum in the Soviet

Embassy in Kabul.[55] In retrospect, it seems most probable that the primary loyalties of the three were less to any Afghan political faction or personality than to the USSR.

Apparently Amin acted swiftly to neutralize Watanjar, Gulabzoy, and Mazdooryar as soon as he became aware of the plot against him. His informant in this case was almost surely his chief of security, Major Sayed Daoud Taroon, who had accompanied Taraki throughout his trip to Havana, and who therefore was probably involved in (or became aware of) the Moscow discussions on removing his chief.

On September 14, Taraki telephoned Amin and summoned him to the presidential palace. Amin must have been reluctant to go, for it was necessary for Soviet ambassador Puzanov, who was present with Taraki, to take up the telephone and assure Amin of safe conduct. Amin then agreed to come, but he was obviously still suspicious, for he and his escort, including Major Taroon, were all armed. As they entered the building, they fell into an ambush, and at least four of the escort, including Taroon, were killed. Amin, however, fought his way clear and survived unscathed.[56]

The failed ambush sealed Taraki's fate. With the key ministries of defense, interior, and communications in the hands of Amin's cohorts, there was no possibility of staging a coup against him. Taraki's only chance for survival would have lain in making his way to the Soviet Embassy to join his three ex-ministers, but Amin must have reckoned with this possibility and lost no time in having him arrested.

Amin's government never did reveal Taraki's arrest, but the following day, September 15, it announced the appointment of new ministers to the posts previously held by Watanjar, Gulabzoy, and Mazdooryar.[57] Gunfire and explosions were heard in Kabul immediately thereafter, apparently indicating that these personnel decisions were being vigorously, if unsuccessfully, disputed. Those opposed to the government's action were subsequently referred to as "some enemies of the people (who) have been eliminated."[58]

On September 16 the *Kabul Times* announced Taraki's retirement from the political scene and Amin's takeover of Taraki's responsibilities. It also reported Taroon's September 14 "martyrdom" and subsequent burial with full honors. On September 18, the other three known "martyrs" were also identified. They were: Nawab (deputy chief of intelligence), engineer Khair Mohammed (president of the "Afghan Construction Unit"), and—conceivably accompanying Amin in anticipation of the need for swift medical treatment for a variety ot assassination techniques—Dr. Sur Gul Khataz (president of preventive medicine in the Ministry of Public Health).

That same day Ambassador Puzanov, in what must be one of the most flagrant recorded instances of diplomatic hypocrisy, publicly signed the condolence book for Taroon.[59]

On September 19, Brezhnev and Kosygin sent their congratulations to Amin, and the latter's triumph appeared to be complete.[60]

Following the announcement of his resignation, Taraki's name was eclipsed from the Afghan media. There was to be only one exception. On October 10, the *Kabul Times* carried the following article (quoted here in full) on its final page, near the bottom:

TARAKI DIES OF ILLNESS
Kabul Oct 10 (Bakhtiar) — Noor Mohammed Taraki, former President of the Revolutionary Council, died yesterday morning of serious illness, which he had been suffering for some time.

The body of the deceased was buried in his family graveyard yesterday.

That was the total obituary coverage of a man whose titles alone had taken almost as many lines in news stories until three weeks before the announcement of his death.

The second Afghan leader in eighteen months had died violently at the hands of his successor. The third had less than three months to live before suffering the same fate.

CHAPTER

8

The Final Months
September–December 1979

. . . One can rarely see neighborliness without some clashes, tensions, and misunderstanding. However, in connection with the DRA and USSR such things have never happened and we are sure that they will never happen in the future. . . . Of course the main and important reason behind this friendship and mutual understanding lies in the fact that the two nations have the greatest respect to vital principles of good relation between nations which are respect to independence, sovereignty, territorial integrity and mutual cooperation without any conditions and strings. . . .

(*Kabul Times* editorial "DRA-USSR friendship treaty," December 6, 1979.)

If the reported date of Taraki's death (the night of October 8–9) is accurate, it had taken Amin three weeks to reach the decision to do away with his rival. During this time he had had to weigh a number of factors: (1) Soviet complicity in the abortive ambush against him and their clear preference for Taraki over him; (2) Soviet denial of any knowledge of the whereabouts of Watanjar, Mazdooryar, and Gulabzoy, all of whom were known (or at least strongly presumed) to be sheltered in the Soviet Embassy; and (3) the continued presence in Afghanistan of the large military delegation under Pavlovskiy. Amin had to reckon with the danger that the liquidation of Taraki might provoke the Soviets into taking decisive action against him. On the other hand, he could scarcely afford to let the former "Great Leader" remain alive and perhaps become the nucleus of a new opposition to his rule.

In 1980 Taraki's murder, by strangulation and suffocation, was de-scribed in grisly detail in the published confessions of Amin's lieutenants.[1] This seems convincing refutation of earlier reports in Western media that he had died of gunshot wounds received in the shootout.[2]

Congratulatory telegrams on his accession to power that poured in from almost all chiefs of state in the Soviet bloc during the last part of September probably contributed to Amin's confidence.[3] So, in all likelihood, did the fact that the USSR itself signed various aid and trade agreements during this period and into October.[4] And perhaps most significant of all to Amin, the Pavlovskiy delegation finally completed its visit and returned to the USSR.[5]

Whatever Amin's considerations, he disposed of his rival with a minimum of fanfare, and appeared to emerge the clear victor. Nonetheless, his position was not an enviable one. There remained only about half of his army's normal officer corps strength of eight thousand; the rest had been killed or had gone over to the rebels. Mutinies in his forces had become commonplace. The PDPA, halved by the excommunication of the Parchamis in 1978, was now splitting again as Amin's supporters ranged against those of Taraki. Insurgency was everywhere; the government could control individual cities by dispatching its dwindling military forces to the most critical danger points, but not even Kabul was safe from insurgent attacks and military rebellions. Afghanistan's economy was in a shambles. And looming over other considerations was the all-too-evident military solution that the USSR might seek to impose if the Afghans failed to set their own house in order.

Amin's response to this situation was to placate as many of his immediate and potential enemies as he could without at the same time weakening his political position by making real concessions. To mollify the Soviets, he commuted the still-pending death sentences of Kisht-mand and Qader to fifteen years imprisonment, and he kept up a steady drumfire of pro-Soviet propaganda in the official Afghan media. Relations between the two countries, he was to tell an American novelist in November, were "based on profound ideological roots."[6] In anticipation of the Soviet National Day (November 7), the *Kabul Times* again referred to Afghanistan's role as a "continuation of the Great October Revolution."[7]

For his domestic audience, propaganda during October and November addressed both internal and external problems in about equal measure without ever quite admitting that they existed. The messages were aimed primarily at dampening the insurgency.

There were periodic reports of the release of hundreds of prisoners from various jails in various parts of the country. (This had been an intermittent propaganda theme since the summer of 1978, and Amin revived it.) Such reports never gave the names of those released or the crimes for which they had been arrested; but the overall impression was one of jails being emptied of all their inmates, who now no longer posed a threat to society.[8]

Claims were made that the government was in favor of "complete freedom of religion and profound respect to Islam and a widescale support thereto. . . ." but these claims were accompanied by demands that "religious fanaticism" be wiped out.[9]

Amnesty was offered for those who had "abandoned their homeland" (i.e., fled to Pakistan or Iran); these offers were accompanied by interviews with happy returnees.[10]

There were, however, some jarring notes as well, particularly as Amin's position vis-à-vis the insurgency continued to deteriorate. In November and December there was a spate of articles dealing with the "voluntary" requests for extension of service by individual soldiers and whole units, to "defend the revolution" or "to fight bandits."[11]

In addition, there was one article that highlighted a heretofore largely unpublicized collectivization effort.[12] This was a drive that could not have been at all popular among Afghanistan's individualistic farmers, many of whose fathers had fled collectivization in Soviet Central Asia. The November 6 timing of this article may indicate that it was intended more to impress Afghanistan's Soviet mentors on the eve of the October Revolution holiday than any domestic audience.

Although there was no interruption in the stream of panegyrics offered up to the Soviet Union, most notably on November 7 but also at other times,[13] a close observer would have noted that only Foreign Minister Shah Wali, not Hafizullah Amin, attended the National Day ceremonies at the Soviet Embassy. Ambassador Puzanov was still in place, and Amin had reason to treat his invitations with some circumspection. (On November 22, Puzanov left Afghanistan permanently, allegedly in compliance with Amin's complaint concerning his September activities.)[14]

Similarly, in an exchange of telegrams on the occasion of the first anniversary of the Soviet-Afghan Friendship Treaty (December 6, 1979), Amin's congratulations went personally to Brezhnev and Kosygin, while their telegram, though addressed to Amin, sent greetings to the "Central Committee, Revolutionary Council, and government of the DRA," but not to Amin personally.[15]

Despite the concentration of lavish praise on the USSR, there began to appear on the back page of the *Kabul Times* a slow but perhaps significant trickle of articles concerning aid donations by the West. Such aid had never ceased entirely, even during 1978: the Afghans had no reason to turn down unencumbered donations, and the West wanted to keep alive at least an implicit Afghan debt of gratitude.

Some of the aid did not seem to serve the West's best interests. For example, a September 1978 DM 1,000,000 grant-in-aid to the Afghan ministry of interior from the Federal Republic of Germany was described as being intended for "technical affairs." The Afghan signatory was Major Taroon, the security chief, who had a reputation for torturing prisoners and who was to die at Amin's side a year later in the shootout with Taraki's backers. The funds were used to support and equip Taroon's secret police, whose avowed task was to protect the Revolution at all costs.

Other grants, however, had humanitarian impact. The Saudis, for example, had extended $5,000,000 for flood relief in September 1978; the following month a 1977 West German DM 45,000,000 loan for economic development and medical aid was changed to a grant-in-aid.[16]

In October 1979 the *Kabul Times* contained articles on the delivery of a DC-10 to Ariana Afghan Airlines, and on a U.S. AID grant.[17] In November there were stories (some accompanied by photos) about American chargé d'affaires Bruce Amstutz giving a $109,844 check to Minister of Education Mohammed Salem Masoodi for use on school buildings, the British ambassador presenting a donation of books, the U.S. sale of cotton ginning equipment, and other similar stories.[18] All such stories continued to appear on the back page, however.

In November there was even a hint that Amin might be trying to mend relations with Iran. In contrast to vitriolic anti-Khomeini editorials that appeared in October, Amin refused comment on Iran to an American interviewer because he was "trying to build fences."[19]

Another noticeable feature of the Afghan press, as autumn turned toward winter, was the growth of Amin's own personality cult. Although he did not assume the "Great Leader" title assumed by Taraki, and although articles decrying the latter's cult (without ever mentioning his name) were common,[20] Amin's cult offered, if anything, a more flagrant warping of reality than his predecessor's. The same practice of including all of his party and state titles at the first mention of his name was a carry-over from Taraki, and Amin's was now the ubiquitous portrait that was shown suspended on every official's wall. He injected a new dimension in cult photography, however: the selective enlargement of his head when he was portrayed in a group. At first only slightly noticeable, the differential in size between him and those with whom he was conferring gradually became grotesque, with the ultimate effect of making him seem a giant among pygmies.[21]

By the end of November Amin's situation was critical, even though he appeared to have fought his internal enemies (excluding the anticommunist insurgents) to a standstill. In mid-October he had survived a coup attempt that seemed to combine the forces of the extreme political right and those of the ousted pro-Soviet left. The latter were represented by an army unit, loyal to Major Watanjar, that was stationed near Kabul and that attempted to mutiny on October 14 or 15.[22]

The political right was the "Afghan Mellat," a political party that dated from the 1960s and promoted national democratic socialism. Although ostensibly in favor of constitutional monarchy at that time, the main planks of its platform—racially oriented nationalism, jingoistic territorial ambitions (it wished to restore Afghanistan to its eighteenth-century borders), and implacable hatred for the West—had more in common with Nazi doctrine than with democracy. It reportedly attempted a coup at the same time as the army unit, and in about the same area. Amin arrested its leaders, the seventy-five-year-old Ghulam Mohammed Farhad and his immediate male relatives, including Qudratullah Haddad, the former editor of the Afghan Mellat's journal, also called *Afghan Mellat.*[23]

It is perhaps tempting to see in the highly chauvinistic, virulently anti-American *Afghan Mellat* an organ that was secretly under Soviet control in the years before Daoud suppressed all private press activity. It would not be the first example of Soviet manipulation of ostensibly far-right organs to promote communist goals. According to one former Afghan government official, however, Ghulam Mohammed Farhad concentrated his published xenophobia on the United States because it was a safer target than the USSR. He detested the USSR with even greater vigor, but dared not say so except in private, because of the proximity of the USSR and the influence wielded by leftist groups in Afghanistan.[24]

Why were the Soviets so bent on removing Amin? They have never admitted complicity in his removal in the first place, but have supported Babrak's accusations, which range from the hypocritical to the absurd, e.g., that Amin was cruel, that he was an agent of the CIA, and that he was trying to strike some kind of bargain with the Pakistanis. Of these, only the first is undeniable. The second is patently false, and the third is open to question.

Amin's real sin in Soviet eyes, however, may have been a refusal to accede to demands that he invite Soviet troops to quell the resistance. For the USSR to have overlooked the possibility for a bona fide invitation seems most unlikely. The difference between an intervention that has been sanctioned and even requested by a chief of state, and one that must be extended *ex post facto* by a successor who has been installed by the intervening force is the difference between true fraternal assistance and an outright military invasion. It is possible that the USSR tried to work out some arrangement with Amin as early as September, following Taraki's ouster but before his murder. If so, Amin appears to have rejected the suggestion. He remained, as we have noted, outwardly loyal to the USSR, but he could not have had a great deal of confidence in their good faith after the September ambush.

Months before that episode, the Soviets had been laying the groundwork for intervention. In late May 1979, following Yepishev's visit, Moscow began referring to Afghanistan as a member of the "socialist community," a designation that covers Warsaw Pact nations plus Cuba, Vietnam, and Mongolia. This served implicit warning that the Brezhnev Doctrine could be invoked in Afghanistan, that is, that Soviet forces could be sent into Afghanistan to "protect socialism," as they had been in Czechoslovakia. (Unfortunately, this designation, though correctly interpreted by many, passed without a fittingly strong U.S. official reaction—indeed without any apparent reaction at all).[25] Thus the ideological groundwork was laid. From that point on, regardless of what the rest of the world might think, a Soviet invasion would be legal from the Soviet standpoint.

The physical preparations for such an event had also been going on for some time. An invasion on the scale of the one launched in late December is not something that one improvises on short notice. There were indicators of unusual military activity that should have been noted and placed correctly in their Afghan context long before the December 22 troop deployments that finally led to a futile public U.S. warning to the USSR. Starting in late October and early November, there were reports of Soviet Central Asian troops being moved into the country in small units and taking over some guard functions from Afghan forces. This was ostensibly a move to free the Afghan troops for combat with insurgents, but its real purpose was to control vital invasion routes.[26]

In late November, Soviet troops were put in a state of limited readiness, and reservists were called up to fill out understrength combat divisions in the Central Asian Military District. Bridging equipment was moved to the Afghan border; Marshal Sergey L. Sokolov set up his headquarters at Termez, just over the border from Afghanistan; and the Warsaw Pact countries placed their forces on an advanced state of readiness.[27]

About mid-December, the Soviets airlifted one or two battalions of troops with heavy weapons (armor and artillery) into Bagram Air Base, whose management (despite Amin's earlier denials) they had been steadily usurping from the Afghans over the preceding months. None of the above provoked any known U.S. protest. As noted subsequently by one journal,

> The U.S. State Department, having had enough controversy about Soviet units and their capabilities for one year (*author's note:* i.e., the furor over the Soviet combat brigade in Cuba), refused to characterize the new force as "combat troops."[28]

That these preparations were going forward on a massive scale does not prove that the USSR had abandoned the idea of persuading Amin to sanction the intervention; they merely reflect the Soviet determination to ensure military success whether Amin concurred or not. From the standpoint of world reaction, it was still patently in Soviet interests that an invitation from Amin be secured.

On November 28, 1979, a Soviet deputy minister of interior, Lieutenant General Viktor Semenovich Paputin, arrived in Kabul for official discussions on "mutual cooperation and other issues of interest."[29] The normal practice with high-level visits of this nature is to publicize them immediately; in this case there was a delay of three days before the *Kabul Times* printed the story, along with a fuzzy picture of

Paputin (in dark glasses), his entourage, and the Afghan welcoming delegation. Discussions with Afghan officials (Paputin's official host was Afghan deputy minister of interior Ghulam Mustafa) reportedly began on November 30, and on December 1 he was guest of honor at a dinner hosted by Kabul Province Governor Shah Nawaz. On the first day of the 1978 coup, Amin had appointed Mustafa as one of the two commanders of the Fifteenth Armored Division and Shah Nawaz as chief of the Commandos. The choice of Paputin's escorts thus appears not to have been fortuitous; Amin had good reason to want to have trustworthy subordinates monitoring Paputin's activities. On December 3 there was a front-page picture of Paputin being received by Amin (the latter reduced to real-life dimensions in this photo) at the People's House in Kabul.

At this point there was a hiatus in press coverage of the visit. On December 8 there was a brief note of a Politburo meeting that dealt with security affairs and an accompanying two-sentence observation that Paputin had met with Minister of Interior Faqir Mohammed Faqir. The next mention of Paputin was on the sixteenth, when the paper reported his departure three days before, "after holding friendly talks with the sources concerned" (not further elaborated). The photo that accompanied the story again portrayed a dim figure in dark glasses surrounded by large and serious Europeans, as well as some Afghans.[30]

In light of the story that was to break later, there was some question whether Paputin really departed Kabul as reported, whether he returned with the Soviet invading forces, and in either case what the nature of his final departure from Afghanistan had been. For his obituary referring to his "untimely" death on December 28, 1979, (place unnamed) was to be published in *Pravda* and *Sovetskiy Sport* on January 3, 1980.

Of the three stories that were to emerge on the manner of his passing, one had him killed on December 27 in yet another firefight with the redoubtable Amin, one had him mortally wounded in such an encounter,[31] and the third (probably Soviet-inspired) alleged that he had committed suicide in Moscow's Sheremetevo Airport on his return from Kabul, as a result of depression at having failed in his mission. In the first two versions, Paputin's mission was allegedly to convince Amin that the latter's personal salvation, as well as that of Afghanistan, rested on his inviting Soviet troops to put down the insurgency. In the third version, his mission was to protect Amin, who was nevertheless

killed "by mistake" in an accidental firefight that broke out at the
Darulaman Palace.[32] However Paputin met his end, it seems to have
been a violent one and directly connected with the equally violent
death of Amin.

Meanwhile, from the middle of December on, Soviet intentions
were emerging ever more unmistakably. Amin's nephew, Assadullah Amin, who was chief of the intelligence service, was seriously
wounded in an assassination attempt in the presidential palace on
December 17. He was evacuated for medical treatment to Tashkent,
from which he returned six months later to face execution for treason
by the Babrak government.[33]

On December 18 and 19 the Soviet contingent that had arrived at
Bagram in mid-December was deployed along the road to the Salang
Pass in order to clear the way for the 357th Mechanized Rifle Division,
which was slated to come in from the north.[34] Close behind them at
Bagram came a parachute regiment that landed on December 21–22.[35]

Apparently recognizing the vulnerability of the downtown Kabul
presidential palace where his nephew had been wounded, Amin
moved on December 22 to Darulaman Palace, a more easily defensible
installation.[36] Later there were to be a number of bizarre reports on the
circumstances surrounding his move to Darulaman Palace, including
one report that had him going into seclusion after being voted down by
his own Central Committee, who wanted to invite Soviet intervention.
This story was doubtless nurtured by the Soviets themselves, but if it
had been true, they would have been the first to identify all such
Central Committee members who had voted for intervention. In fact,
those members of Amin's Central Committee who survived the invasion and the first rounds of Babrak executions soon fell into total
eclipse.

The day that Amin moved to Darulaman Palace, Washington finally
broke its silence on developments in Afghanistan and along the USSR's
Afghan border. Previous airborne landings, plus the presence of thirty
thousand Soviet troops in a high state of readiness on the Afghan
border could no longer be ignored.[37]

Whether any U.S. warning, whenever tendered, would have deterred Moscow is doubtful; but in any case, by December 22 the
momentum of the Soviet commitment was probably irreversible. Late
on Christmas Eve the first elements of an airborne assault began
landing at Kabul International Airport.

It was a well-planned, well-executed operation, one that reportedly involved several elements of sabotage and deception:

• Soviet advisors to tank forces in and around Kabul saw to it that batteries were removed from all vehicles, allegedly in order to replace them with cold-resistant, winterized ones. This removed one of the greatest hazards to the airborne operation that brought Soviet infantry directly to Kabul via the civilian airport. Just a few tanks on the runways would have frustrated this move.[38]

• The central communications complex for the government, managed by the Afghan air force, was taken over and its key officials were killed by a Soviet commando team.[39] The key figure in this operation was no less than the Soviet minister of communications himself, Nikolay Vladimirovich Talyzin. He arrived in Kabul early on December 24 for a "friendly visit," accompanied by a large retinue of burly, unsmiling aides.[40] With such a prestigious visitor on hand, the whereabouts of all key Afghan communications officials would be known to the Soviets, and the doors of otherwise closed and guarded installations would be open to the visitors.

• Arriving simultaneously with Minister Talyzin was the Uzbek SSR's minister of water resources. On December 27, he and Talyzin cohosted at the Intercontinental Hotel a large reception to which leading Afghan dignitaries were invited. At the end of the festivities the guests were all arrested.[41]

• Also on the evening of December 27, Afghan officers of the Kabul garrison were invited to an early cocktail party hosted by their Soviet military colleagues. At 6:30 P.M. most of the Soviet officers quietly departed, leaving behind copious supplies of liquor. Shortly thereafter, as explosions sounded outside, the Afghans tried to leave but found themselves locked in.[42]

Without communications, it must have been some time before Amin realized what was happening. When he did, there was no longer any opportunity for effective resistance. Throughout Christmas Day, AN-12 and AN-22 transports had been landing and taking off at Kabul airport at ever shorter intervals. From nightfall, December 25 on, flight density at the airport reached one in every three minutes; five thousand troops were landed by the evening of December 26.[43] Afghan officials apparently thought that the new troops were coming in as part of an authorized build-up, and there was no resistance. When Soviet troops finally went into action, their numbers and firepower were overwhelming.

H-hour was 7:15 P.M. on December 27. The Soviet troops that had been airlifted into Kabul made a coordinated attack on key government installations. Simultaneously two or three battalions, spearheaded by light tanks, struck at Darulaman Palace. In contrast to the almost total lack of opposition elsewhere, Amin and his guard put up staunch resistance and were only overcome shortly before midnight. The wing of the palace where they made their stand was completely destroyed, and all of the defenders were wiped out. For their part, the Soviet attackers lost several vehicles and about twenty-five killed and two hundred twenty-five wounded.[44] It is probably safe to assume that Amin himself personally accounted for some of these casualties; he was a good shot.

The following day, two motorized rifle divisions crossed the land frontier in three places to support the troops that had been airlifted. By January 1, 1980, fifty thousand Soviet troops were in Afghanistan and more were on the way. Four motorized infantry divisions were deployed along the Soviet-Afghan border, providing a reserve of another fifty thousand men.[45]

Amin had been a merciless Marxist dictator, whose jailers and firing squads were rarely underemployed; but there was no question as to his bravery under fire. Whatever his other characteristics, his country owes him one debt of gratitude: he never tendered the Soviets the key invitation that would have legalized the invasion. He paid for that refusal with his life.

CHAPTER
9

Aftermath and Recommendations

There is no necessity to insist on the palpable interest of Russia in restricting the growth of her territory and preventing the advent of complications in distant provinces which may retard and paralyze our domestic development.

(From a Prince Gorchakov memorandum of November 21, 1864, in relation to Russian expansion towards Khiva. Quoted in W. Fraser-Tytler, *Afghanistan*, p. 336)

From 1978 on, events in Afghanistan unfolded with a certain inevitability. Those familiar with the country knew beforehand that no communist government could survive there without massive outside support; but the intensity, persistence, and pervasiveness of the resistance came as a surprise even to many Afghans. Through 1978 and 1979 these qualities called forth ever greater political and military countermeasures from the Taraki and Amin governments and from the USSR. These, in turn, only stiffened the opposition. In the end, the Soviet invasion, prompted by a gamut of ideological and strategic factors, was undertaken in order to provide the ultimate *force majeure* solution, one that had already been successfully employed in Eastern Europe.

It has not worked in Afghanistan, where opposition has only spread, sharpened, and solidified. The remains of the Afghan army have become totally unreliable from the Soviet standpoint; the PDPA continues to be riven by the Parcham-Khalq rivalry (the blood-feud nature of which intensified throughout 1980); and the government has been reduced to a largely clerical function, with Soviet officials making all decisions and countersigning all orders. The population-at-large, in spite of mass reprisals, continues to support the insurgency. Soviet forces control only limited areas for limited time periods, and these revert to insurgent domination when the troops leave. Even in Kabul itself, resistance activities such as strikes, bazaar closures, and student demonstrations (to say nothing of individual assassinations of government officials and Soviet troops) were chronic features of the 1980 scene. No end of trouble is in sight.

Some of the Soviet calculations and miscalculations of the costs of their Afghan adventure can be conjectured with confidence:

Suspension of the U.S. administration's efforts to push Salt II through the Senate   This was a predictable, almost inevitable, price that would have to be paid. Inasmuch as chances for ratification appeared small anyway, it was a sacrifice the Soviets were willing to make.

Suspension of American scientific and technological exchanges   Although in the long run this might cause some problems, the USSR could feel reasonably sure that American willingness to hold firm would erode, just as it had with sanctions taken after Czechoslovakia and other Soviet foreign adventures. In the meantime, Soviet espionage could provide a substitute for open exchanges.

Halting American wheat shipments   Again, this was a possible penalty that probably would last only a short time. It doubtless occurred to Soviet American experts that the American president would find it hard to hold firm to such a policy in an election year. That the policy did continue to hold, and that the USSR suffered yet another bad harvest year as well, were complications that were probably not anticipated.

Further development of U.S. rapprochement with China   Of all the arguments likely to have been raised in opposition to the invasion, this would have carried perhaps more weight than any other. The fact that it did not deter the USSR from proceeding as planned may be ascribed to Soviet miscalculations as to the strength of both Chinese and American reactions, as well as a miscalculation of the Soviet ability to complete their operation as swiftly as planned.

Negative world reaction   This has surely been more intense than the Kremlin anticipated. Similar Soviet actions in Eastern Europe did not provoke nearly the storm the attack on Afghanistan did. The Third World's interest in European conflicts (involving states on both sides that were relatively rich) was far less intense than their concern with a fellow emerging nation. The 104 to 18 UN General Assembly vote condemning the invasion was the worst diplomatic defeat suffered by the USSR since the Korean War.

Olympics boycott   This U.S. option may not even have occurred to Soviet leadership. If the possibility was considered, it was probably ruled unlikely for a number of reasons: a recent history of U.S. vacillation in the foreign policy field, the heavy influence of sport in the United States, and (again) the fact that in an election year the American president would be unlikely to offend such a significant voting block as athletes and fans.

Poland   The extent to which the Afghan resistance has inspired the Polish workers to defy their own government (and through it the Kremlin) can only be guessed. This was a cost the USSR could not have reckoned with.

While the United States can take some credit for making the USSR pay more heavily than it anticipated, the major credit must go to the Afghans themselves. Their implacable hatred of foreign domination and their willingness to sacrifice property and lives to fight against it were new phenomena for the Soviet army. The smaller countries of Eastern Europe—fought over, conquered, and occupied by Great Powers for generation after generation—have been more or less accustomed to the experience of being dominated. Whatever their true feelings, considerations of sheer survival have dictated some measure of caution in dealing with large conquerors. These countries are also relatively rich, with multiple, overlapping organizations; good communications; and built-in levers of control. None of this is true of Afghanistan, where the resistance fighter and his forebears have never in tribal memory been occupied by foreigners except for the briefest of interludes, where there is little of economic value to lose by fighting, where organizations (aside from the family/tribe) are almost nonexistent, and where the basic units of opposition are single, indomitable individuals, not malleable groups.

Perhaps the single most significant result of all of these factors was the failure of the USSR to conquer the country swiftly and present the world with a *fait accompli*. Had it succeeded in doing so, the various reprisal measures taken by the United States and others would likely have eased as anticipated, and Afghanistan would have become just another fading memory, like Hungary and Czechoslovakia. Instead, Afghanistan has continued to defy conquest, whatever the odds, and there is no end in sight for the occupation force's troubles.

The USSR has not been alone in overestimating its own capabilities and underestimating those of the resistance. Throughout 1980 responsible Western newspapers predicted crushing, decisive Soviet offensives "when the snows melt," "after the Olympics," and "when winter sets in." None of these predictions has come true. Meanwhile, those search-and-destroy missions the Soviets have attempted have met with only qualified success.

On the other hand, although the costs of the invasion and occupation have been unquestionably higher than anything anticipated by the Kremlin, there are no signs of any Soviet intention to withdraw. Clearly, to the Soviet leaders the price of retreat appears to be potentially even greater than the ongoing drain of men, materiel, and prestige that Afghanistan is exacting. The potential penalties of retreat include the possible spread of the Islamic nationalist contagion into Soviet Central Asia and the weakening of the Soviet hold on Eastern Europe, as well as the surrender of a strategically valuable stepping stone toward domination of Middle East oil resources. It can be predicted that the overall costs to the USSR of continued occupation will have to rise considerably before the Soviets will risk exacerbating such problems. At the same time, the very intensity and duration of the Afghan resistance have already denied them any kind of secure base in the country and the spirit of resistance is threatening to spread to other areas under Soviet domination.

It is significant that the USSR has been careful to preserve for itself the option of retreat. The consistent Soviet line has been that its "limited military contingents" would be withdrawn as soon as all forms of "outside interference" in the country ceased. When the USSR chooses to decide that the alleged interference has ceased, it can so declare and leave. (The objective existence or absence of any such interference is largely immaterial to Soviet decision-makers.) It is probably significant that Afghanistan is not yet a member of the Warsaw Pact.

Unfortunately, however, no early decision to leave appears very likely at this time, and the toll of death and misery continues to rise in the country. For those who know and love that land and its people, it is not a pretty picture to contemplate.

Did the United States go wrong in its policies, and if so where? What can be done to encourage a Soviet pullout? What might be done to avoid similar situations elsewhere in the future? This exercise in hindsight is not intended to give offense to those former colleagues in the American Embassy in Kabul and in Washington who, to greater and lesser degrees, share with me the responsibility for not having seen clearly then what seems so obvious now.

In judging these questions, one must differentiate between the period prior to May 1978, the 1978–79 era, and the post-invasion phase. It is also necessary to put Afghanistan in context with various perceptions of the worldwide balances of forces, and the limitations that American public opinion puts on the exercise of national power.

The American neo-isolationism that followed the Vietnam tragedy left countries like Afghanistan even more vulnerable to outside aggression than before. At the same time, the USSR perceived itself as achieving military parity and, before long, military superiority over the United States. That perception, in turn, has led to the emergence of a new Soviet aggressiveness and willingness to take risks the likes of which have not been seen since the days of the Nazi-Soviet pact.

Before the 1978 communist coup, however, the Soviet commitment in Afghanistan was minimal. If that coup had failed, the USSR would have totaled up its losses (with or without noisy propaganda) and waited for the next opportunity. It is virtually certain that there would have been no Soviet military intervention to support the PDPA at that time. The best time for the United States to have taken preventive measures would have been before May 1978; thereafter, most options were closed and the Soviet commitment became increasingly difficult to reverse.

During Daoud's 1973–78 stewardship of Afghanistan, U.S. policies were by and large the best that could have been applied, given the environment and the lack of domestic American enthusiasm for foreign involvements. Our aid projects, although severely restricted in comparison with those of earlier years, were long-term and generally successful, including a little-known but widely appreciated textbook program for primary and secondary schools. Had we been in a position to increase aid dramatically (without a corresponding willingness to undertake strategic commitments in the country), it would probably only have provoked the USSR into moving against Daoud even earlier.

One of the key developments that preceded the 1978 coup, however, was the June 1977 reconciliation of the Parcham and Khalq factions of the PDPA. That should have sounded warning bells in Washington, for it should have been obvious to analysts of Afghanistan that this was no freely achieved political compromise in the Western sense of politics, but an imposed union that overrode deep-seated antagonisms. Only one outside force could have dominated the mutual distrust that Parcham and Khalq felt for one another: the fount of ideology to which they both owed allegiance—the CPSU. If that fact had been recognized, then questions should have been asked concerning the significance that should be attached to that reconciliation in terms of Soviet intentions. It might not have been possible to arrive at a firm answer to these questions, but at the very least there should have been an intensified effort to learn what the newly unified PDPA was up to.

Assuming that that information was acquired, that it was correctly assessed, and that there was a recommendation to act on it, what could have been done? In earlier years the United States might have considered setting up or supporting some kind of internal counterforce to offset the growing threat from the left; or it might have increased foreign aid sharply in an attempt to alleviate dissatisfactions that gave the left new adherents. Neither of these would have been a viable option in Afghanistan in the late 1970s. Foreign aid was increasingly difficult to obtain from the American congress, and "meddling in internal affairs" of foreign lands was becoming extremely unpopular among the American electorate.

The only counterforce that could have thwarted the PDPA was Daoud himself. *If* we did have the information (and we should have had it), and *if* we did assess it correctly (as we should have), some way should have been found to put it in Daoud's hands without compromising the means by which it was acquired. Had that been done, it is likely that the coup of April 27, 1978, would not have occurred.

Once the coup had taken place, U.S. options were severely restricted. The temptation to provide military support to Afghan insurgents who were fighting the Taraki and Amin regimes was resisted.

This withholding of aid was painful but it was the correct decision in light of the subsequent developments. Had there been such U.S. support, there would have been a very significant body of opinion in the United States and throughout the world that it was only U.S. "meddling" that prompted the Soviets to invade. In such circumstances, our own determination to take countermeasures after the invasion would have been severely weakened, as Soviet propaganda (which has tried vainly to sell this line) correctly perceived.

Again, however, there should have been adequate appreciation of the Soviet intention to invade, and there should have been at least some U.S. action to try to modify that intention. One indication, as we have noted, was the declaration in late May 1979 that Afghanistan was now a "member of the Socialist family of nations." This designation should have been vigorously protested by the United States, which should have pointed up its significance to other UN members. An attempt should have been made to force the USSR into defining whether or not the doctrine of limited sovereignty applied in the case of Afghanistan, and when that demand was met (as it surely would have been) with equivocation, the United States should have made an issue of that fact too. By itself, such U.S. maneuvering would not have deterred the USSR, but if nothing else, it might have given the Kremlin a foretaste of the negative world reaction in store for it after the invasion.

By the same token, there is cause for concern in the failure of the United States to react effectively to obvious Soviet preparations for invasion until those preparations had reached an irreversible stage. (It is tempting, perhaps, to see in this failure a Machiavellian plot deliberately to involve the USSR with the Afghan tarbaby in order to sap Soviet energies in a far-off region of minor intrinsic importance to the United States. Happily, the conduct of our foreign affairs has a long way to go to reach such depths of sophisticated perfidy.)

According to subsequent accounts, during the last weeks of 1979 the United States delivered to the USSR no fewer than five warnings against invading. Only the December 22 warning was made public at the time and Soviet preparations went ahead undeterred. That the first such warning should be unpublicized was perhaps warranted. Thenceforth, however, the United States should have focused world attention on the Soviet preparations and started to mobilize international resistance to it.

Today, with Afghanistan under Soviet occupation, U.S. options, paradoxically, have widened. At this point the matter of foreign intervention is no longer nearly so sensitive: the Soviets themselves have set the precedent, freeing our own hands for following suit if we so desire. The only question is whether, if we give arms to the Afghan insurgents, such aid should be open or discreet—whether it should be overtly associated with the United States or simply appear, unattributed, on the scene. In this regard, the routes by which the arms might reach Afghanistan must be considered. Those nations bordering Afghanistan (Pakistan, China, and Iran) all have their own internal and external problems that would affect possible deliveries. The credibility of U.S. commitments to stand by its international obligations is also of key importance. If the countries through which arms transit have reason to feel that the United States is not steadfast in its commitments (and there have been, regrettably, instances of such perceptions), their willingness to permit such activities will be less than enthusiastic.

This begs the basic issue, however. *Should* the United States arm the insurgents? There are those who claim that this will inevitably lead us into a greater and greater commitment to the insurgents, into the introduction of U.S. advisors, and finally into the commitment of U.S. combat forces in a confrontational situation with Soviet forces. It need not be so. We can and should draw the line at any direct U.S. involvement.

On the other hand, we should indeed see to it that the Afghans receive weapons, especially the surface-to-air missiles that will help neutralize the helicopter gunships. The Afghans will go on fighting anyway, with stones if necessary, and we should not deny them the opportunity to be more effective. To those who might not regard this as a moral obligation, there is an argument of cold logic: the more expensive we make it for the Soviets in Afghanistan today, the less likely they are to undertake similar adventures elsewhere in the future.

A separate question is whether this aid should be overt. Here the very discussion of the problem can be somewhat sensitive. Rather than go into details, we will confine ourselves to the recommendation that aid be afforded to the Afghans with neither confirmation nor denial that it originates from the United States. The corollary recommendation holds that if it comes to a conflict between secrecy and efficiency, efficiency should prevail. Security considerations should neither unduly limit nor significantly delay arms aid. (In this regard, it is to be hoped that U.S. officials can regain their right and courage to respond to probing journalistic questions with a simple "no comment" answer when appropriate—a capability that seems to have been largely lost in recent years.)

A more problematic question is whether the United States should take any action to try to heal the splits between the various mutually antagonistic Afghan resistance groups. Unlike Parcham and Khalq, with their Soviet ties, none of these groups owes allegiance to any foreign power, least of all to the United States; and our ability to apply leverage, even if we wanted to, is severely circumscribed. It is nowhere near as great, for example, as the Soviet capability to force a Parcham-Khalq reunion, an effort that, as we have seen, was only very briefly effective anyway.

On the other hand, the military capabilities of the resistance are badly weakened by the continued bickering among the various groups, undoubtedly spurred on with considerable enthusiasm by PDPA and Soviet agents who have penetrated them. The policy of the United States should be to expose any such machinations of the agents whenever and wherever we can and also to discourage even unprovoked factional activities by pointing the finger of suspicion at all who practice them. Identifying and highlighting factionalism as a Soviet aim should help reduce it within the resistance.

The great strength of the resistance—proud, independent individualism—is also its greatest weakness, preventing the kind of compromise necessary to form strong organizations. Hopefully in the long run, the overriding nature of the Soviet threat will produce unification; if so, it will probably come about with the emergence of some new charismatic resistance leader. Until that day comes, the United States should take only a relatively passive, advisory role in promoting union, while at the same time exposing all who would prevent it.

Still another option for the United States—and one that again touches on a basic conflict between security and efficiency—is to make the world aware to the fullest degree possible of what is going on inside Afghanistan. This means declassifying and making public current intelligence about the country. Among the most critically important audiences are those in the USSR and in Afghanistan itself. Although rigorous Soviet censorship prevents any free exchange of news, modern communications do get through, and information spreads in the Soviet bloc despite all means taken to halt it. Recalling the effect of pictorial information (especially television coverage) on U.S. politics during the Vietnam era, no effort should be spared to acquire accurate, vivid illustrations of combat horrors in Afghanistan and to expose Soviet and other foreign audiences to them. Obviously this cannot be in the form of television, but even still photographs can be effective.

That the demands of the Afghan occupation are worsening the already extremely difficult food and consumer goods situation in the USSR is clear. The patience of the Soviet body politic is enormous, but it is finite, and the United States should not hesitate to make clear for Soviet audiences the connection between domestic shortages and the Afghan adventure. In the end, domestic unrest in the USSR may prove to be more effective in blunting Soviet aggressive foreign policies than any outside pressure.

The Afghan audience should get its own due share of attention. If reports are true that Iranian announcers speaking Iranian Farsi instead of Afghan Dari are being used on Voice of America broadcasts to Afghanistan, this practice should be done away with forthwith. Afghans have a well-honed mountaineer's contempt for flatlanders, and the Iranian accent is unmistakable. Afghan audiences deserve Afghan announcers.

Furthermore, it should be U.S. presidential policy to express on a repeated and consistent basis our moral support for the Afghan insurgency and our condemnation of the continued Soviet occupation. The USSR counts on the inability of the United States to hold to any position over the long term. In the case of Afghanistan, the USSR must be disabused of this belief, and reminded periodically of our own and the world's contempt for their aggression.

There are those who will argue that the USSR cannot afford to appear to give in to U.S. pressure, that we ought to provide a "graceful escape route" for them. The USSR has shown an ability in the past to put on a given Soviet act any interpretation that it feels is appropriate. (The very invasion of Afghanistan is a case in point.) It needs no "ladder" of our manufacture with which to extricate itself. While it may be in U.S. interests to vary the degree of pressure we apply from time to time (and perhaps to indicate a willingness to let up if there are reliable indications of a Soviet intention to pull out), we should not feel obligated to concern ourselves with Soviet sensitivities to an excessive degree.

At the same time we should also disabuse the USSR of any fears that a vengeful Afghanistan, with or without U.S. support, will become its blood enemy and attempt to stir up trouble in Soviet Central Asia. The Afghans cannot afford to have permanently bad relations with the USSR, any more than they could afford permanent hostility toward Britain before 1947. The illustrations of Afghan adherence to their treaties with Britain when the latter was in serious trouble (e.g., during the Indian Mutiny of 1857, World War I, and World War II) should be adequate proof of this thesis.

Finally, we should make it abundantly clear to all concerned (to Afghans at least as much as to Soviets) that we have no intention whatsoever of supplanting the USSR in terms of trying to manage the country. The United States has no interest in seeing Afghanistan revert to anything but its traditional role as a nationally free, truly non-aligned, and independent country.

That policy should be clearly and specifically enunciated and repeated. If it is eventually realized, we will have done a service not only for Afghanistan but, in the long run, for ourselves as well.

Notes

Notes to Chapter 1

1. Quoted in A. Evelyn Ashley, *The Life of Lord Palmerston*, vol. 2 (London: R. Bentley and Son, 1876), p. 25. Cited in Vartan Gregorian, *The Emergence of Modern Afghanistan* (Stanford: Stanford University Press, 1969), p. 102.

2. Abdur Rahman Khan, *The Life of Abdur Rahman Khan, Amir of Afghanistan*, vol. 2, ed. Sultan Mohammed Khan (London: J. Murray, 1900), p. 280. Quoted in Louis Dupree, *Afghanistan* (Princeton: Princeton University Press, 1973), p. 415.

3. Vartan Gregorian, *The Emergence of Modern Afghanistan* (Stanford: Stanford University Press, 1969), p. 132.

4. Ibid, pp. 203–204.

5. Ibid.

6. A. C. Jewett, *An American Engineer in Afghanistan*, ed. Marjorie Jewett Bell (Minneapolis: University of Minnesota Press, 1948), pp. 303ff. See also Gregorian, *Modern Afghanistan*, p. 205.

7. Gregorian, *Modern Afghanistan*, p. 220. The characterization of the three factions is his.

8. Ibid., p. 226.

9. *Kabul Times*, August 3, 1978.

10. Ibid., August 7, 1978.

11. Gregorian, *Modern Afghanistan*, p. 226. The original source is listed as "The War in Afghanistan," *Labour Monthly* 2, no. 3 (March 1929): 181.

Notes to Chapter 2

1. V. M. Vinogradov, et al., eds., *Sovetsko-afganskiye otnosheniya 1919–1969*, (Moscow: Politizdat, 1971), p. 7.

2. Ibid., pp. 11–12.

3. Ibid., pp. 8–9.

4. Ibid., pp. 10–11.

5. Vartan Gregorian, *The Emergence of Modern Afghanistan* (Stanford: Stanford University Press, 1969), p. 232.

6. *The Truth About Afghanistan—Documents, Facts, Eyewitness Reports* (Moscow: Novosti Press Agency Publishing House, 1980), p. 23.

7. Georges Agabekov, *OGPU: The Russian Secret Terror* (New York: Brentanos, 1931), p. 46. Agabekov personally hand carried the first million rubles to Kabul in 1924.

8. Vinogradov, *Sovetsko-afganskiye otnosheniya*, pp. 11–12.

9. Gregorian, *Modern Afghanistan*, p. 474.

10. Ibid., pp. 235, 474.

11. Ibid., p. 232. Gregorian is citing Louis Fischer, *The Soviets in World Affairs*, vol. 1 (London: J. Cape, 1930), p. 286.

12. S. I. Ozhegov, *Slovar russkogo yazyka*, 10th ed. (Moscow: Izdatelstvo "Sovetskaya Entsiklopediya," 1973).

13. Yu. A. Polyakov and A. I. Chugunov, *Konets basmachestva* (Moscow: Nauka Press, 1976), p. 3.

14. Hélène Carrère d'Encausse, *L'Empire Éclaté* (Paris: Flammarion, 1978), p. 26.

15. Polyakov and Chugunov, *Konets basmachestva*, p. 44.

16. Ibid., pp. 79–80, 84, and 127–28, for example. Soviet authors have no reason to emphasize such matters, but are clearly aggrieved by the duplicity of the locals.

17. *San Francisco Chronicle*, September 3, 1980.

18. Polyakov and Chugunov, *Konets basmachestva*, pp. 93–95.

19. Ibid., p. 55.

20. Gregorian, *Modern Afghanistan*, p. 232.

21. Ibid.

22. Polyakov and Chugunov, *Konets basmachestva*, p. 67.

23. Ibid., p. 90.

24. Ibid., pp. 70–71.

25. Fitzroy MacLean, *Eastern Approaches* (London: J. Cape, 1949), p. 146; Robert Conquest, *The Great Terror* (New York: Macmillan, 1968), pp. 516–19.

26. Polyakov and Chugunov, *Konets basmachestva*, p. 101.

27. *The Truth About Afghanistan*, p. 24.

28. Polyakov and Chugunov, *Konets basmachestva*, pp. 40, 168–69.

29. Ibid., pp. 93–94.

30. Vinogradov, *Sovetsko-afganskiye otnosheniya*, p. 29.

31. Guenther Nollau and Hans Juergen Wiehe, *Russia's South Flank* (New York: Praeger, 1963), p. 98.

32. Ibid., p. 101.

33. Gregorian, *Modern Afghanistan*, p. 238.

34. Ibid.

35. Ibid., p. 255, and Louis Dupree, *Mahmud Tarzi: Forgotten Nationalist*, American Universities Field Staff Report (AUFS) South Asia Series, vol. 8, no. 1, January 1964, LD–1–64, p. 2.

36. Louis Dupree, *Afghanistan's "Big Gamble," Part I: Historical Background of*

Afghan-Russian Relations, American Universities Field Staff Report (AUFS), South Asia Series, vol. 4, no. 3, April 1960, LD–3–60, p. 13.

37. Vinogradov, *Sovetsko-afganskiye otnosheniya*, p. 45.

38. Polyakov and Chugunov, *Konets basmachestva*, p. 131.

39. Agabekov, *OGPU*, pp. 86–93.

40. Dupree, *Afghanistan's "Big Gamble" Part I*, AUFS, LD–3–60, p. 13.

41. Agabekov, *OGPU*, pp. 158–70, and Gregorian, *Modern Afghanistan*, pp. 278–79. The sources are divided on the question of whether Ghulam Nabi's forces were defeated in the field or whether they voluntarily withdrew from a militarily winning position because of Amanullah's abdication.

42. Polyakov and Chugunov, *Konets basmachestva*, pp. 138–39. The Soviet authors of course also lay a good deal of blame for the Basmachi on foreign intrigues, but it is obvious that Afghanistan was too beset with domestic problems for such meddling, while Britain, with the onset of the depression, was scarcely in a position to foment rebellion so far from home.

43. Ibid., p. 164.

44. Dupree, *Afghanistan's "Big Gamble": Part I*, AUFS, LD–3–60, p. 14.

45. Gregorian, *Modern Afghanistan*, p. 338.

46. Agabekov, *OGPU*, pp. 86–93.

47. An uncertain but intriguing indicator of possible clandestine Soviet connections with Ghulam Nabi is provided by recent Afghan historiography. Shortly after the April 1978 coup, the *Kabul Times* began a series of articles on Afghan history that was to run at least until the end of the year and was clearly designed to rewrite the historical record according to "correct" ideological precepts. Though Ghulam Nabi features prominently as a martyr to Nader Shah's bestiality (*Kabul Times*, June 21, 22, and 23, 1978; the prose is extravagantly lurid), parts of his background are strangely obscured: for example, his biography mentions an earlier diplomatic tour in Moscow in the early 1920s but nothing about his presence in the USSR in 1929, even though he was ambassador there at the time. There is no mention whatsoever of his march into northern Afghanistan, and no effort is made either to deny or to detail the subversive activities for which he was executed. It is almost as if a carefully sanitized dossier had been made available to the propagandist whose duty it was to write the articles.

48. Louis Dupree and Linette Albert, eds., *Afghanistan in the 1970s* (New York: Praeger, 1974), p. 30.

49. Ibid.

50. Ibid.

51. Louis Dupree, *Red Flag over the Hindu Kush—Part I: Leftist Movements in Afghanistan*, American Universities Field Staff Report, Asia 1979, no. 44, September 1979, LD–2–79, p. 17.

Notes to Chapter 3

1. Louis Dupree, *Afghanistan* (Princeton: Princeton University Press, 1973), p. 480.

2. Ibid., p. 481.

3. Vartan Gregorian, *The Emergence of Modern Afghanistan* (Stanford: Stanford University Press, 1969), pp. 389–91.

4. Peter Franck, *Afghanistan Between East and West* (Washington, D.C.: National Planning Association, 1960), p. 6.

5. Ibid., p. 37.

6. Ibid., pp. 36–45.

7. Dupree, *Afghanistan*, pp. 499–507; Franck, *Between East and West*, p. 66.

8. Louis Dupree, *Afghanistan's "Big Gamble": Part II—The Economic and Strategic Aspects of Soviet Aid*, American Universities Field Staff Report (AUFS), South Asia Series, vol. 4, no. 4, May 1960, LD–4–60, p. 6.

9. Dupree, *Afghanistan*, p. 492.

10. Ibid., p. 491.

11. Ibid., p. 512.

12. V. M. Vinogradov, et al., eds., *Sovetsko-afganskiye otnosheniya 1919–1969* (Moscow: Politizdat, 1971), p. 7.

13. Dupree, *Afghanistan*, p. 493.

14. Vinogradov, *Sovetsko-afganskiye otnosheniya*, pp. 110–12.

15. Dupree, *Afghanistan's "Big Gamble": Part II*, AUFS, LD–4–60, p. 7.

16. Ibid.

17. Franck, *Between East and West*, p. 9.

18. *The Truth About Afghanistan—Documents, Facts, Eyewitness Reports* (Moscow: Novosti Press Publishing House, 1980), p. 30.

19. Louis Dupree and Linette Albert, eds., *Afghanistan in the 1970s* (New York: Praeger, 1974), p. 44.

20. Dupree, *Afghanistan*, pp. 510–11.

Notes to Chapter 4

1. Louis Dupree, *Afghanistan* (Princeton: Princeton University Press, 1973), pp. 494–95.

2. Louis Dupree, *Afghanistan's Slow March to Democracy*, American Universities Field Staff Report (AUFS), South Asia Series, vol. 7, no. 1, January 1963, LD–1–63, p. 12.

3. Dupree, *Afghanistan*, p. 495.

4. Richard S. Newell, *The Politics of Afghanistan* (Ithaca: Cornell University Press, 1972), p. 66.

5. V. M. Vinogradov, et al., eds., *Sovetsko-afganskiye otnosheniya 1919–1969* (Moscow: Politizdat, 1971), pp. 113–14.

6. Peter Franck, *Afghanistan Between East and West* (Washington, D.C.: National Planning Association, 1960), p. 55.

7. Ibid. Interestingly, this agreement is not included in the compilation of Soviet-Afghan agreements listed in Vinogradov, *Sovetsko-afganskiye otnosheniya*.

8. Dupree, *Afghanistan*, p. 513.

9. Franck, *Between East and West*, p. 56.

10. Ibid., pp. 12–13.

11. Dupree, *Afghanistan*, p. 522.

12. W. Fraser-Tytler, *Afghanistan* (London: Oxford University Press, 1967), p. 321.

13. Louis Dupree, *Afghanistan's "Big Gamble": Part II—The Economic and Strategic Aspects of Soviet Aid*, American Universities Field Staff Report (AUFS), South Asia Series, vol. 4, no. 4, May 1960, LD–4–60, p. 7.

14. Franck, *Between East and West*, p. 12.

15. Dupree, *Afghanistan*, p. 507. Dupree's figure of 3600 miles for this road seems excessive.

16. Franck, *Between East and West*, p. 12.

17. Vinogradov, *Sovetsko-afganskiye otnosheniya*, pp. 115–17.

18. Dupree, *Afghanistan*, p. 508.

19. Ibid., p. 499.

20. Louis Dupree and Linette Albert, eds., *Afghanistan in the 1970s* (New York: Praeger, 1974), p. 43.

21. Vinogradov, *Sovetsko-afganskiye otnosheniya*, pp. 122–25.

22. Ibid., pp. 125–27.

23. Dupree, *Afghanistan*, p. 518.

24. Ibid., p. 508.

25. Franck, *Between East and West*, p. 57.

26. Vinogradov, *Sovetsko-afganskiye otnosheniya*, pp. 129–34.

27. Louis Dupree, *American Private Enterprise in Afghanistan: The Investment Climate, Particularly as It Relates to One Company*, American Universities Field Staff Report (AUFS), South Asia Series, vol. 4, no. 9, December 1960, LD–9–60, p. 4.

28. Franck, *Between East and West*, p. 461.

29. Vinogradov, *Sovetsko-afganskiye otnosheniya*, pp. 127–29.

30. Dupree, *Afghanistan*, pp. 514–22.

31. Franck, *Between East and West*, pp. 45–46.

32. Ibid., p. 72 (quoting *Mutual Security Act of 1958*, Hearings, vol. 2, p. 1707).

33. Ibid., p. 67; Newell, *Politics of Afghanistan*, pp. 128–29.

34. Franck, Newell, Dupree, et al. reached this conclusion.

35. Dupree, *Afghanistan's "Big Gamble": Part II*, AUFS, LD–4–60, p. 3.

36. Vinogradov, *Sovetsko-afganskiye otnosheniya*, pp. 185–86.

37. Franck, *Between East and West*, p. 65.

38. Vinogradov, *Sovetsko-afganskiye otnosheniya*, p. 156.

39. Ibid., pp. 179–82.

40. Personal conversations with the author by both engineers and attachés.

41. Dupree, *Afghanistan*, p. 511.

42. Louis Dupree, *The Mountains Go to Mohammed Zahir—Observations on Afghanistan's Reactions to Visits by Nixon, Bulganin-Khrushchev, Eisenhower, and Khrushchev*, American Universities Field Staff Report (AUFS), South Asia Series, vol. 4, no. 6, May 1960, LD–6–60, p. 25.

43. Franck, *Between East and West*, p. 12.

44. Fraser-Tytler, *Afghanistan*, p. 322.

45. Ibid., p. 323.

46. Dupree, *Afghanistan*, p. 539.

47. Ibid., pp. 544–45.

48. Louis Dupree, *"Pushtunistan"—The Problem and Its Larger Implications*, American Universities Field Staff Report (AUFS), South Asia Series, vol. 5, no. 1, October 1961, LD–1–61, p. 11.

49. Dupree, *Afghanistan*, p. 541.

50. Dupree, *"Pushtunistan,"* LD–1–61, p. 10.

51. Fraser-Tytler, *Afghanistan*, p. 326.

52. Louis Dupree, *The Decade of Daoud Ends: Implications of Afghanistan's Change of Government*, American Universities Field Staff Report (AUFS), South Asia Series, vol. 7, no. 7, May 1963, LD–7–63, p. 3.

53. Ibid., p. 6.

54. Ibid., p. 11.

Notes to Chapter 5

1. Louis Dupree and Linette Albert, eds., *Afghanistan in the 1970s* (New York: Praeger, 1974), p. 54. The simile is from a former cabinet minister.

2. Louis Dupree, *An Informal Talk with King Mohammed Zahir of Afghanistan*, American Field Staff Report (AUFS), South Asia Series, vol. 7, no. 9, July 1963, LD–9–63, p. 3.

3. Louis Dupree, *Constitutional Development and Cultural Change—Part III: The 1964 Afghan Constitution (Articles 1–56)*, American Field Staff Report (AUFS), South Asia Series, vol. 9, no. 3, September 1965, LD–3–65, p. 17.

4. Louis Dupree, *Afghanistan* (Princeton: Princeton University Press, 1973), p. 590.

5. G. Grassmuck, L. W. Adamec, and F. H. Irwin, eds., *Afghanistan—Some New Approaches* (Ann Arbor: University of Michigan Press, 1969), p. 171.

6. Dupree, *Afghanistan*, p. 497.

7. Grassmuck, *Afghanistan—Some New Approaches*, p. 170.

8. Dupree, *Afghanistan*, p. 497.

9. Louis Dupree, *Red Flag over the Hindu Kush—Part I: Leftist Movements in Afghanistan*, American Universities Field Staff Report (AUFS), Asia 1979, no. 44, September 1979, LD–2–79, p. 6.

10. Peter Franck, *Afghanistan Between East and West* (Washington, D.C.: National Planning Association, 1960), pp. 10, 72.

11. "The Revolution in Afghanistan," *The New Left Review*, no. 112 (November–December 1978), p. 22.

12. Ibid.

13. Dupree, *Afghanistan*, pp. 591–92.

14. Ibid., p. 649.

15. R. T. Akhramovich, *Outline History of Afghanistan After the Second World War* (Moscow: Izdatelstvo vostochnoy literatury, 1966), p. 183.

16. R. T. Akhramovich, *Afganistan v 1961–66 gg.* (Moscow: Nauka, 1967), p. 183.

17. Grassmuck, *Afghanistan—Some New Approaches*, pp. 184–85.

18 Dupree, *Afghanistan*, pp. 596–97.

19. Louis Dupree, *Afghanistan: 1966*, American Universities Field Staff Report (AUFS), South Asia Series, vol. 10, no. 4, July 1966, LD–4–66, p. 12.

20. Ibid.

21. Dupree, *Afghanistan*, pp. 602–603.
22. Dupree, *Afghanistan: 1966*, AUFS, LD–4–66, p. 13.
23. Dupree and Albert, *Afghanistan in the 1970s,* p. 62.
24. Dupree, *Red Flag—Part I*, AUFS, LD–2–79, pp. 7, 9.
25. *Kabul Times*, July 5, 1978.
26. Richard S. Newell, *The Politics of Afghanistan* (Ithaca: Cornell University Press, 1972), p. 144.

Notes to Chapter 6

1. Louis Dupree, *A Note on Afghanistan: 1974*, American Universities Field Staff Report (AUFS), South Asia Series, vol. 18, no. 8 (Afghanistan), September 1974, LD–4–74, p. 1.

2. Louis Dupree, *Red Flag over the Hindu Kush—Part I: Leftist Movements in Afghanistan*, American Universities Field Staff Report (AUFS), Asia 1979, no. 44, September 1979, LD–2–79, p. 7.

3. *Kabul New Times*, May 8, 1980.

4. Dupree, *Afghanistan: 1974*, AUFS, LD–4–74, p. 19.

5. Dupree, *Red Flag—Part I*, LD–2–79, p. 12.

6. Dupree, *Afghanistan: 1974*, AUFS, LD–4–74, p. 2.

7. Louis Dupree, *Afghanistan* (Princeton: Princeton University Press, 1973), pp. 757–58.

8. Ibid.

9. Dupree, *Red Flag—Part I*, AUFS, LD–2–79, p. 9.

10. Ibid., p. 10.

11. Louis Dupree, *Toward Representative Government in Afghanistan—Part I: The First Five Steps*, American Universities Field Staff Report (AUFS), Asia 1978, no. 1, February 1978, LD–1–78, p. 10.

12. Dupree, *Red Flag—Part I*, AUFS, LD–2–79, p. 10. In an earlier description of this event, Dupree hinted that Maiwandwal might have been murdered and that he was an anathema to leftists; in the work cited here, the murder allegation is explicit, and though Dupree's term for the unidentified murderers ("extreme leftists") remains undefined in this case, the widespread Parcham penetration of the Ministry of Interior (under whose aegis Maiwandwal was being held) provides circumstantial evidence that Parcham was responsible.

13. Dupree, *Toward Representative Government*, AUFS, LD–1–78, p. 1.

14. Dupree, *Afghanistan: 1974*, AUFS, LD–4–74, p. 19.

15. Dupree, *Red Flag—Part I*, AUFS, LD–2–79, p. 12. Dupree lists Abdulellah along with Hassan Sharq as someone with close connections to Parcham but who was probably not a member. Whatever his ideological bent, Abdulellah was not widely respected in the Daoud cabinet; his appointment was commonly ascribed to family loyalty, his father having been a close friend and confidant of the man who raised Daoud and Naim after their father's assassination.

16. Conversations in 1980 with a former ranking U.S. Embassy official. Several ranking Afghans had told him privately of Jalalar's undeclared pro-Soviet orientation.

17. Dupree, *Red Flag—Part I*, AUFS, LD–2–79, p. 13.

18. Ibid. Dupree (without citing his sources) states that these individuals were all recruited into Khalq by Taraki (sic) only in 1977. Inasmuch as all three vanished under the Khalq regime of Hafizullah Amin in 1979 and emerged as ministers only after Soviet forces returned the Parchami Babrak to power, it seems likely that their primary allegiance was to Parcham, if not (as seems most likely of all) directly to the USSR. If this is the case, one must also question the year 1977 as the date of their recruitment to a pro-Soviet cause; it probably occurred earlier, most likely during their training in the USSR.

19. Dupree, *Toward Representative Government*, AUFS, LD–1–78, pp. 7–9.

20. Dupree, *Afghanistan: 1974*, AUFS, LD–4–74, p. 9.

21. Louis Dupree, *Red Flag over the Hindu Kush—Part II: The Accidental Coup, or Taraki in Blunderland*, American Universities Field Staff Report (AUFS), Asia 1979, no. 45, September 1979, LD–3–79, p. 1.

22. Louis Dupree, *Afghanistan 1977: Does Trade Plus Aid Guarantee Development?* American Universities Field Staff Report (AUFS), South Asia Series, vol. 21, no. 3, August 1977, LD–3–77, p. 4.

23. Louis Dupree, *Toward Representative Government in Afghanistan—Part III: Steps Six Through Nine—and Beyond?* American Universities Field Staff Report (AUFS), Asia 1978, no. 14, February 1978, LD–2–78, pp. 1–3.

24. Private conversation with a member of Daoud's extended family in 1979. The source had heard this directly from Naim on the latter's return from Moscow. Naim was concerned that Daoud did not seem to sense the depth of Soviet ire that he (Naim) had detected.

25. Dupree, *Red Flag—Part I*, AUFS, LD–2–79, p. 11.

26. Dupree, *Red Flag—Part II*, AUFS, LD–3–79, p. 1.

27. Ibid, p. 4.

28. *Keyhan* (Tehran), April 29, 1978.

Notes to Chapter 7

1. *International Herald Tribune*, May 2, 1978.

2. *On the Saur Revolution*, The Political Department of the People's Democratic Party of Afghanistan in the Armed Forces of Afghanistan (Kabul, May 22, 1978), p. 11.

3. Ibid., p. 12.

4. Ibid., p. 21.

5. Ibid., p. 4.

6. Louis Dupree, *Red Flag over the Hindu Kush—Part II: The Accidental Coup, or Taraki in Blunderland*, American Universities Field Staff Report (AUFS), Asia 1979, no. 45, September 1979, LD–3–79, p. 6.

7. *Daily Telegraph*, May 4, 1978; *Financial Times*, May 4, 1978.

8. *Daily Telegraph*, May 4, 1978.

9. *Kabul Times*, May 3, 1978.

10. *On the Saur Revolution*, p. 12.

11. Dupree, *Red Flag—Part II*, AUFS, LD–3–79, p. 5.

12. Ibid.

13. *On the Saur Revolution*, p. 14.

14. Ibid., pp. 17–19.

15. Ibid., p. 28.

16. Dupree, *Red Flag—Part II*, AUFS, LD–3–79, p. 14.

17. *International Herald Tribune*, February 24–25, 1978.

18. Ibid., May 2, 1978.

19. Ibid., May 5, 1978.

20. *The Guardian*, May 8, 1978.

21. Dupree, *Red Flag—Part II*, AUFS, LD–3–79, p. 13. Amin was later to raise this figure to 101.

22. Personal conversation with a former prisoner who had talked with Republican Guard prisoners before their execution.

23. *Kabul Times*, November 28, 1978.

24. Dupree, *Red Flag—Part II*, AUFS, LD–3–79, p. 14 and Louis Dupree, *Red Flag over the Hindu Kush—Part I: Leftist Movements in Afghanistan*, American Universities Field Staff Report (AUFS), Asia 1979, no. 44, September 1979, LD–2–79, p. 13. Dupree avers that in 1973 Qader was a "non-leftist coup participant." If so, he became a convert not too long thereafter. It is more probable that he came under Soviet influence earlier, during training in the USSR.

25. *On the Saur Revolution*, p. 29.

26. *Kabul Times*, August 6, 1978.

27. *Daily Telegraph*, August 18, 1979.

28. *Kabul Times*, September 23, 1978. There were eight pages instead of the usual four in this issue.

29. Ibid.

30. Ibid.

31. Ibid., May 6, 1978; May 7, 1978; and May 15, 1978, for example.

32. "Nightmare in Baluchistan," *Foreign Policy*, no. 32, Fall 1978, pp. 136–60.

33. See "Afghan Tribesmen in Revolt," *Daily Telegraph*, June 5, 1978, for an early description of the process of disaffection in the countryside.

34. *Kabul Times*, September 24, 1978, and September 25, 1978, for example; many other examples were to follow.

35. Ibid., November 26, 1978.

36. Ibid., October 26, 1978.

37. *Kabul Times*, December 9, 1978. This article was later used to justify the Soviet invasion.

38. *The Economist*, January 13, 1979.

39. *The Truth About Afghanistan—Documents, Facts, Eyewitness Reports* (Moscow: Novosti Press Agency Publishing House, 1980), p. 42.

40. *International Herald Tribune*, April 14–15, 1979.

41. *Daily Telegraph*, March 29, 1979.

42. *International Herald Tribune*, March 29, 1979.

43. Ibid., April 14–15, 1979.

44. *Christian Science Monitor*, February 4, 1980.

45. *International Herald Tribune*, August 7, 1979.

46. Ibid., August 13, 1979.

47. "The Soviet Military Stake in Afghanistan 1956–79," *Journal of the Royal United Services Institute for Defence Studies* 125, no. 3 (September 1980): 35.

48. "Die Intervention in Afghanistan—das Ende der Sowjetischen Koexistenzpolitik?" *Berichte des Bundesinstituts fuer ostwissenschaftliche und internationale Studien*, no. 6 (1980), p. 4.

49. *The Economist*, January 5–11, 1980.

50. *The Guardian*, October 29, 1979.

51. *The Economist*, November 3, 1979.

52. *New York Times*, September 20, 1979.

53. *Kabul Times*, September 16, 1979.

54. Ibid., September 12, 1979.

55. *The Economist*, November 3, 1979.

56. Ibid.

57. *Kabul Times*, September 15, 1979.

58. Ibid., September 18, 1979.

59. Ibid., September 17, 1979.

60. Ibid., September 19, 1979.

Notes to Chapter 8

1. *Kabul New Times*, January 27 and 28, 1980. This paper is the replacement for the *Kabul Times*, which ceased publication with the Soviet invasion.

2. *New York Times*, September 19, 1979.

3. *Kabul Times*, September 20, 22, 24, and 30, 1979.

4. Ibid., September 24; October 6 and 7, 1979.

5. "The Soviet Stake in Afghanistan," *Journal of the Royal United Services Institute for Defence Studies* 125, no. 3 (September 1980): 35. The stay of the delegation in Afghanistan lasted for nearly two months according to this source, indicating that it would have departed in early October.

6. *Kabul Times*, November 25 and 26, 1979.

7. Ibid., October 29, 1979.

8. Ibid., October 3, 1979, for example.

9. Ibid., October 11, 1979.

10. Ibid., October 2, 1979.

11. Ibid., November 17 and 21, 1979.

12. Ibid., November 6, 1979.

13. Ibid., November 7 and 8, 1979.

14. Ibid., November 22, 1979.

15. Ibid., November 25, 1979.

16. Ibid., September 16, 1979.

17. Ibid., October 8 and 15, 1979, respectively.

18. Ibid., November 17, 18, and 26, 1979, respectively.

19. Ibid., November 25, 1979.

20. Ibid., November 18, 1979.

21. Ibid., October 25, 1979; November 5, 13, and 21, 1979.

22. *New York Times*, October 17, 1979; Dupree, *Afghanistan* (Princeton: Princeton University Press, 1973), p. 612.

23. *New York Times*, October 16, 1979.

24. Conversation with Dr. Sarwar Nassery, former Afghan Foreign Office official, in early November 1980.

25. *Daily Telegraph*, June 2, 1979.

26. "The Soviet Military Stake in Afghanistan: 1956–79," *Journal of the Royal United Services Institute for Defence Studies* 125, no. 3 (September 1980): 35–36.

27. Ibid.

28. Ibid.

29. *Kabul Times*, December 1, 1979.

30. Ibid., December 16, 1979.

31. *Foreign Report*, no. 1614 (January 9, 1980), pp. 1–2.

32. *Washington Post*, February 18, 1980. This story appeared first in the *London Observer* on February 17. It is almost certainly a piece of Soviet "disinformation."

33. *The Economist*, June 14, 1980.

34. "The Soviet Military Stake," *Journal of Royal United Services Institute for Defence Studies*, September 1980, p. 36.

35. Ibid.

36. *Kabul Times*, December 22, 1979.

37. *San Francisco Chronicle*, December 22, 1979.

38. "After Afghanistan, What?" *Commentary* 69, no. 4 (April 1980): 47.

39. Personal conversations with an Afghan émigré in January 1980.

40. *Kabul Times*, December 25, 1979.

41. *Le Soir* (Brussels), February 12, 1980.

42. *Newsweek*, January 21, 1980.

43. "Afghanistan—Soviet Occupation," *Background Brief* (Foreign and Commonwealth Office, London), February, 1980.

44. "Afghanistan and the Rule of Law," *The Review* (New York: International Commission of Jurists, June 1980), p. 43.

45. "The Soviet Invasion of Afghanistan," *Backgrounder* (Washington, D.C.: The Heritage Foundation, January 9, 1980), p. 3.

Selected Bibliography

The materials chosen for this bibliography include nonspecialized works of general background interest as well as some items from contemporary journals that put the 1979 Soviet invasion in perspective. Louis Dupree's *Afghanistan* (Princeton: Princeton University Press, 1973, pp.699–720) contains excellent bibliographic information. In addition, Dupree's *Afghan Studies* (American Universities Field Staff Report, Asia Series, vol. 20, no. 4, LD-4-76, November 1976) provides the serious researcher with a comprehensive list of organizations working in the field of Afghan studies.

Adamec, Ludwig W. *Afghanistan 1900–23: A Diplomatic History*. Berkeley: University of California Press, 1967.

————. *Who's Who of Afghanistan*. Graz (Austria): Akademische Druk- u. Verlagsanstalt, 1975.

————. *Supplement to Who's Who of Afghanistan: The Democratic Republic of Afghanistan*. Graz (Austria): Akademische Druk- u. Verlagsanstalt, 1979.

Akhramovich, Roman Timoveyevich. *Afghanistan v 1961–66 gg*. Moscow: Nauka, 1967.

————. *Outline History of Afghanistan After the Second World War*. Moscow: Izdatelstvo vostochnoy literatury, 1966.

Carrère d'Encausse, Hélène. *L'Empire Éclaté—La Revolte des Nations en U.R.S.S*. Paris: Flammarion, 1978.

Charters, David. "Resistance to the Soviet Occupation of Afghanistan." *Conflict Quarterly*, 1 (Summer 1980): 8–15.

Conquest, Robert. *The Great Terror: Stalin's Purges of the Thirties*. New York: Macmillan, 1968.

Dupree, Louis. *Afghanistan*. Princeton: Princeton University Press, 1973. (An insert *Epilogue 1980* is available for contemporary volumes.)

————. American Universities Field Staff Reports (AUFS), South Asia and Asia Series, 1959–1980. Dupree has been the AUFS referent for Afghanistan in this series of monographs.

Dupree, Louis, and Albert, Linette, eds. *Afghanistan in the 1970s*. New York: Praeger, 1974.

Fischer, Louis. *The Soviets in World Affairs*. London: J. Cape, 1930.

Franck, Peter. *Afghanistan Between East and West*. Washington, D.C.: National Planning Association, 1960.

Fraser-Tytler, W. *Afghanistan*. London: Oxford University Press, 1967.

Garrity, Patrick J. "The Soviet Military Stake in Afghanistan: 1956–79." *RUSI— Journal of the Royal United Services Institute for Defence Studies* 125 (September 1980): 31–36.

Grassmuck, G. L.; Adamec, L. W.; and Irwin, F. H., eds. *Afghanistan—Some New Approaches*. Ann Arbor: University of Michigan Center for Near East and North African Studies, 1969.

Gregorian, Vartan. *The Emergence of Modern Afghanistan*. Stanford: Stanford University Press, 1969.

Harrison, Selig S. "Nightmare in Baluchistan." *Foreign Policy*, no. 32 (Fall 1978): 136–59.

Jewett, A. C. *An American Engineer in Afghanistan*. Minneapolis: University of Minnesota Press, 1948.

Kazemzadeh, Firuz. "Afghanistan: The Imperial Dream." *The New York Review of Books*, February 21, 1980: 10–14.

Kielinger, Thomas. "A Soviet Diplomat: We Bridle Slowly But Do Some Fast Riding." *Soviet Press—Selected Translations* (U.S. Air Force publication), 80*3, March 1980: 88–90. The German original of this item appeared in *Die Welt* of January 14, 1980, p. 1.

Klass, R. T. "The Great Game Revisited." *The National Review*, October 26, 1979: 1366–68.

Luttwak, Edward N. "After Afghanistan, What?" *Commentary* 69 (April, 1980): 40–49.

Ministerstva inostrannykh del SSSR i Afganistana. *Sovetsko-afganskiye otnosheniya 1919–69*. Edited by Vinogradov, V. M., et al. Moscow: Politizdat, 1971.

Newell, Richard S. *The Politics of Afghanistan*. Ithaca: Cornell University Press, 1972.

Nollau, Guenther, and Wiehe, Hans Juergen. *Russia's South Flank*. New York: Praeger, 1963.

On the Saur Revolution. Kabul: The Political Department of the Peoples Democratic Party of Afghanistan in the Armed Forces of Afghanistan, May 22, 1978.

Polyakov, Yu. A., and Chugunov, A. I. *Konets Basmachestva*. Moscow: Nauka, 1976.

Smith, Harvey H., et al. *Area Handbook for Afghanistan*. 4th ed., Foreign Area Studies, The American University. Washington, D.C.: U.S. Government Printing Office, 1973.

The Truth About Afghanistan—Documents, Facts, Eyewitness Reports. Moscow: Novosti Press Agency Publishing House, 1980.

Valenta, Jiri. "From Prague to Kabul—The Soviet Style of Invasion." *International Security*, no. 630 (Harvard University Center for Science and International Affairs, Fall 1980): 114–41.

Warhurst, Geoffrey. "Afghanistan—A Dissenting Appraisal." *RUSI—Journal of the Royal United Services Institute for Defence Studies* 125 (September 1980): 26–29.

Index